I Need You to Survive

MICHELLE WARD

/25 W MAPLE ST
MILTON PA

minstrels7@yahoo.com
(570) 850-0130
(570) 742-8668

DEDICATION

I'd like to dedicate this book to the amazing people in my life. To Jim, my loving and loyal husband: I love you and appreciate your endless attention and consistent faithfulness. You stayed by my side every minute of the day and night, even through your own fears and weakest moments. To my great kids, Cheri, Dani, and Aaron, and their wonderful spouses, Mark, Chris, and Amber. I can't conceive how I could have ever made it without your constant care and endless support. Never in a million years would I have imagined that life's "role-reversal" process could have happened this early in my life. You definitely stepped up, and stepped in to take care of your mother, and I love you all the more for it. To my church family and friends: Thank you for your continual prayer, constant encouragement, and countless displays of love. I'm indebted to you for helping me walk through every bend, turn, and dark valley I encountered during this journey. Most importantly, however, I thank my Lord and Savior Jesus Christ. He held onto my hand every day, especially in those rare moments when I did find myself alone and afraid. I've learned so much during this time in my life. It's incredible how He uses people to represent His hands and voice in our lives to build faith, hope, and courage. I love him so much.

CONTENTS

ACKNOWLEDGMENTS

Insert acknowledgments text here. Insert acknowledgments text here. Insert acknowledgments text here. Insert acknowledgments text here. Insert acknowledgments text here. Insert acknowledgments text here. Insert acknowledgments text here. Insert acknowledgments text here. Insert acknowledgments text here. Insert acknowledgments text here.

1 SYMPTOMS

My story began in the spring of two thousand three. I remember like it was yesterday. I spent over eight hours in the emergency room. After a battery of tests and procedures, the doctor cleared her throat and declared, "It's cancer." Assuredly, and without any reserve, the diagnosis of cancer easily slipped through her lips like she was diagnosing an ordinary common cold, poison ivy, or sinus infection. She delivered it in a very "matter of fact" manner. Considering I had no pain, nor any symptoms of the disease, I really couldn't comprehend what she said.

Springtime is so beautiful, my favorite time of year. Trees, grass, and all vegetation that were left pale and colorless from the harsh winter bloom into new and fresh life. From this perspective, one can draw strength and hope for a brighter future.

During the last several months, I struggled with some health problems. My blood pressure, glucose, and cholesterol levels were elevated. I became desperate to see my life move into newness, like the reflection of spring. So, I got serious about my health. I made a New Year's resolution to do something about it.

Good results began to appear immediately after I made a few deliberate and determined changes. I received a clean bill of health from my doctor. I wanted to continue this upward trend, so I added an exercise program to my newly-developed program.

Proper diet started my progress, but walking or riding a bicycle would definitely enhance this good progression. Physical activity had not been a priority in my life. At forty-eight, doctor's orders were to go slow.

My stationary bicycle sat in the family room downstairs for quite a while collecting dust. Excited about this newfound desire, I pulled it out of the corner, cleaned it off, and hopped on. For me, this kind of disciplined, physical training became boring real fast, so I thought I would use this time to strengthen my voice and practice singing.

Everyone loves to sing. That's what I do in life. The Lord gave me a love for music. He also gave me talent to deliver it and the opportunity to perform it. I was constantly searching for new music and performance tracks to use. Now I could rehearse and exercise at the same time.

Every night I turned on the CD player, I got on my bicycle and pedaled to the beat of the music. With each mile achieved, and every word memorized, excitement swelled in my heart. I was proud of my accomplishments. Every night my singing got louder and louder. It filled the house with the same song over and over again!

"Honey, would you please turn the music down a little bit…please?" My

husband moaned from the living room above.

I had disturbed Jim's evening nap on the couch. Anyone else would have thought I was crazy, but after nearly thirty years of marriage my routine habits were quite familiar to him. He always supported my music.

The following night, after my routine ride concluded, I closed up my little studio/gym. I noticed my ankles looked swollen, but didn't think much of it. I finished the evening duties of packing lunches and getting clothes ready, then showered for the night. The next morning my ankles were fine.

Another day passed. I began to really look forward to my new schedule. By now, I had most of the new song memorized and wanted to increase exercise time. However, swelling increased, and now even the calves of my legs appeared thicker. They were so puffy, Jim noticed too.

"That's strange," said Jim. "Maybe one leg, but both? Why don't you call your doctor? You've never had that problem before."

In the morning both legs were fine, but I chose to follow Jim's instruction. I went to see my regular physician. He had no idea what the problem could be. No evidence of swelling was apparent at that time. The only answer he could offer was I must have increased the amount of sodium in my diet.

"Just keep an eye on the type of food you eat", he said.

It sounded like a reasonable explanation, so I dismissed any suspicions I had and my regiment continued. Night after night as I bellowed, "Filled within, free from sin, you've got to be born again!" The funky, country rhythm of the song inspired enthusiasm and made the exercise fun for me. With the new song memorized, I was ready to share it with anyone who had an ear to hear or an open heart to receive it.

However, the joy I experienced by putting those words in my heart faded quickly when I noticed the swelling had spread farther up my legs. An uncomfortable, tight feeling advanced upward, beyond my knees, and into my thighs.

Puzzled about this new development, I made an appointment the next day to see Doctor Simpson. Again, no evidence could be seen. I couldn't convince him how abnormal this swelling was. He insisted sodium in my diet contributed to the condition.

Things did not improve. With each day the swelling got tighter and more painful. I finally had to give up the exercise. At the end of each day I would go straight up to my bedroom and rest, hoping the next morning would be better.

Going back and forth from work to the clinic, I was becoming a nuisance to the staff. Every time I called for another appointment, I could sense they were annoyed with my persistence. They put each call on hold for longer periods of time. Dr. Simpson finally prescribed an ultrasound.

He wanted to make sure there were no blood clots. The test results showed nothing abnormal. I was back to square one with no diagnosis, no prognosis, and no answers.

After another appointment, Dr. Simpson suggested (perhaps guessed?) the swelling could be created because of large varicose veins in my legs. He hadn't noticed them before. He prescribed thigh-high support stockings to wear for the entire day. I agreed to try, but God help the people who have to endure the awful, uncomfortable feeling those stockings cause.

I struggled daily to put them on before going to work. After work, I spent the remaining hours of my day in bed with my feet elevated. Without any relief, the bulging persisted.

This pattern continued for almost three weeks, but it seemed like months. I managed to get to work every day, but cooking, household chores, and regular life as I knew it were no longer options I could perform.

"Don't worry about it," Jim would say, "I know how to do the laundry, and there's always something here to eat."

He remained sweet about it, but I knew fast food, sandwiches, and microwave dinners got old, real fast. Jim's biggest concern wasn't the issue with the food he ate, or the dirty dishes, or the laundry building up. My situation hadn't shown any improvement. We were both worried.

The Easter holiday came fast. Good Friday arrived. My family had a music ministry. We'd been together for twenty-five years. We traveled and ministered often. Our schedule included an engagement for that night. I wasn't physically or emotionally prepared for it.

I'd been at work all day. My legs were puffy, sore, and achy. As soon as I got home, I went straight to bed. I needed to get off my feet for a little while before getting ready to go out. I felt a wave of heat rush through my body as soon as my head hit the pillow.

Jim brought me a thermometer, which verified a temperature of over one hundred degrees. Just a mild fever, but enough for me to question whether or not I should go to the church service.

I already had an appointment for the next day. I could wait until then. At least with a fever added to my symptoms, someone may take me seriously. Dr. Simpson had the weekend off. I would be seeing another doctor. I felt relief. This physician might try a different approach to investigate my condition. But for now, our group promised to participate. The commitment needed to be kept. Even if the doctors didn't know how to fix me up, I trusted the Lord would get me through this night.

Making myself content, I got up and dressed for the evening. The four of us, my husband, his sister, and our daughter, Danielle, usually traveled in the same vehicle, but my daughter decided to drive separately that night. The two of us arrived later at the church, leaving Jim, and his sister, Bek, to take the equipment in and get everything set up. There's a lot of work

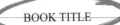

involved in this type of ministry. I felt guilty they didn't get any help from me.

Being an incredibly warm spring night, the church still had a good turn-out for the service. People packed into the small sanctuary like sardines. The stifling heat made me miserable. I felt sick to my stomach. Our selections intertwined between various speakers and presentations. I couldn't slip out early.

"You really look washed out, Hon," Jim said. "How are your legs?"

Fearing I would burst out in tears, I didn't speak, but nodded a weak reply of 'no'.

"Go home, we have things covered here," he said.

I struggled with the decision to go home at the end of the program. There's so much work to do, tearing the equipment down and packing the car, but I knew my temperature had risen. I still felt nauseous, and now had chills. With swollen limbs, their skin stretched tightly and painful, terrible imaginations and fears filled my mind

Tears bobbled at the corners of my eyes, ready to drop with my next move.

I replied, "I hate to leave you and Bek to pack all the stuff up. You've been up since the alarm went off at three o'clock this morning. It's already ten o'clock now, and you're already exhausted."

With his eyes dead set into mine, he declared, "Go home."

"But..."

"No buts about it. Go home with Dani now. You know I don't mind. This is what we do. I like doing it. I'll be fine."

Grateful Dani had driven her car, I reluctantly agreed. When we arrived at my house, she helped me upstairs. Then she gathered extra pillows from the couch in the living room to prop up my legs, and fixed me a nice, ice-cold glass of water.

"I really hate to leave," she said as her voice dropped off. The quiet, unsure tone of her voice indicated her concern.

"No, you have your own family to take care of, but please pray for me before you leave."

Out of our three children, Dani seemed to have the strongest faith. She always studied her Bible, and stayed by my side until the day she married. Hence, she became lovingly known as my "shadow". Her companionship and friendship were so important to me now. Her sweet, soft prayer drifting into my ears felt soothing and comforting.

She sat on the bed with me for a few minutes and said, "Don't worry mom, I'm sure you'll be fine. Do you need anything else right now?"

"No, I'm just glad you could bring me home"....

My voice broke in the middle of the sentence. Regardless how comforting her voice was, I finally lost control of my emotions.

"My God, Dani, what's wrong with me?"

I began to weep, "I don't get it, what's wrong, and why they can't find anything?"

She held me in her arms for a few minutes. We both took a few deep breaths. It worked. Peace set in again.

"Don't worry," she said again. "It'll be okay. I'm sure. I love you. If you need me, just call. I've got to get home." She spoke as she left the room.

"Love you too. I have another doctors' appointment tomorrow. If I find anything out, I'll let you know. Be careful going home," I replied.

The quiet calm began to evaporate once more with each of her fading steps. By the time I heard her drive away, panic hit me in the face like a cement brick. I buried my head in my pillow and drenched it with tears. Why is this happening to me? Discouragement and negative thoughts took over. Doesn't God love me?

I allowed voices of doubt to sink into my mind, and found myself at an all-time low. I tried to pull myself together by remembering God's Word. Scriptures flooded my mind. I forced myself to speak these words out loud, declaring them with boldness:

Isaiah 59:19

...When the enemy shall come in like a flood, the Spirit of the Lord will lift up a standard against him.

2 Timothy 1:7

For God hath not given us the spirit of fear; but of power, and of love, and of a sound mind.

Amazing things happen when the Word of God is spoken. It's as if the elements and molecules absorb the words from the air. Your declaration is miraculously shaped into reality.

It's hard to explain, but in an instant, I sensed a glorious, awesome presence fill the room. The whole atmosphere changed. My spirit changed. A serene calmness ushered out the pain and frustration I felt in that moment. Not only peace came, but also the comfort only Christ can bring. No more confusion. I was back to feeling secure in the love of my Savior.

Problems can seem immense in the middle of the moment, and the mind can imagine situations are worse than they really are. That's why God's Word is so important to help us keep our thoughts under control. It's the stability of the Word that gives us a peace that passes human understanding.

Philippians 4:7

And the peace of God, which passeth all understanding,
shall keep your hearts and minds through Christ Jesus

2 Corinthians 10:5

Casting down imaginations, and every high thing that exalteth itself against the
knowledge of God, and bringing into captivity every thought to the obedience of Christ.

I had to stop, listen, and let God's Spirit minister to me. I had to allow the Lord to help me. I let circumstances sink me into a dark, lonely place. However, His Word brought me back, blocking those negative thoughts. As my fear settled, forcing doubt out, my faith resurrected. I was content with the knowledge I could go through anything with the Lord's help. His comforting presence made the difference. Sleep came quick, and with it the rest I desperately needed.

In the morning I sat in the doctor's office again. My temperature was back to normal, but the swelling persisted from hip to toe.

I welcomed the new face before me as she said, "Hello Mrs. Ward. What's going on with you today?"

Her name was Dr. Read. I tried to explain to her, the best way I could, what happened to my legs. Reviewing my case, she ordered more extensive blood work, and investigated other options like hormonal imbalance and iron levels. Perhaps something was overlooked. Finally, I sensed serious concern from the medical profession toward my condition—Hallelujah!

It didn't take long to get the test results back. My blood count indicated infection somewhere in my body. I had an extreme anemic condition. Thank God, I finally found someone with a fresh outlook on things. At least I had some answers. The anemia concerned me. At least it was something that indicated a problem, and more information than I had received over the last three weeks. She prescribed a daily iron supplement and of course, told me to stay off my feet.

Driving home I realized the next day was Easter; a long day of non-stop standing. We would begin with an early Sunrise service, followed by our traditional Easter Sunday buffet, then a special program in the evening. I needed God's help. Where would all this lead? What was God's plan for me? I looked to His Word for consolation, His Spirit for perfect peace, and His wisdom for assurance.

Proverbs 3:5

Trust in the Lord with all thine heart,
and lean not unto thine own understanding.

2 WAITING

I love Easter. It's the celebration of the risen Christ. The gospel signifies the death, burial, and resurrection of Jesus Christ. That's what I sing about. Without it, there is no song, and no joy.

The holiday came. Even though I loved rejoicing with my friends at church and receiving the Holy Sacrament of communion, I faced a long, trying day.

Sunrise Service started bright and early. I managed to arrive on time despite the challenges I faced. Latecomers began to filter in within the hour. The sanctuary soon became enveloped with a sweet, welcoming Spirit.

We had a brief service with a few special songs, and a message from Pastor. Then everyone went to breakfast at a local restaurant. We were all glad the drive to the breakfast was only five minutes, because by that time everyone was hungry. In the face of my situation, this warm, beautiful, sunny day presented a refreshing distraction for me.

Nestled beside a small pond, complete with fresh, green foliage and a white, wooden, octagonal gazebo, the restaurant had an aura of primitive country. Easter eggs, bunnies, and flowers, plants, and greens were tastefully displayed throughout the building. This was accompanied by all the beautiful pastel colors of spring. The large stone fireplace in the center of the dining room set a wholesome stage for a warm, friendly atmosphere in which to sit down and kick your shoes off.

Because my circumstances seemed so bleak and miserable, I needed this diversion. The colors, aromas, and the spirit of the atmosphere certainly helped get my mind off myself for a while. We shared hearty fellowship, great food, and warm, inspiring conversation together.

After breakfast we all returned to church for the main event of our celebration. Our church had grown by leaps and bounds, and this day was evidence of that. Filled to capacity, the congregation flowed out into the halls, down the steps, and into the Sunday School rooms. Extra monitors were there to view the service.

Praise and worship boomed. I tried to concentrate on the service, but with each passing moment it became more difficult. The longer I stood, the tighter I could feel the skin around my calves and thighs stretching, itching, and burning. As much as I loved the service, I couldn't wait to get home and off my feet.

Pastor delivered an awesome message. The choir blessed us all. At the end of the program I almost collapsed. I couldn't hide my condition any more. I sat down on the steps of the platform. Some dear friends knelt beside me and prayed.

The minute we all got home I sought relief. Right inside the front door sat our most comfortable sofa. I never got past that point. I stayed there for the rest of the day. That's when the kids realized their mother was going through something serious. There was never an Easter when I didn't prepare a large family meal. Sitting on the couch, I felt so guilty.

"Sorry," I told them. "I just didn't have it in me to cook a big spread today. I did put a small ham in the oven earlier, so that will have to do."

Amber, my new daughter-in-law, poked her head around the corner of the kitchen.

"Don't worry," she said, "I made sweet potato casserole last night. I will throw some macaroni and cheese together."

Aaron, my son, chimed in and said, "Yeah, and I picked up some rolls and goodies for us. We'll be fine. Just sit there and relax. We'll fix your plate for a change."

I thought to myself, now that's a real treat.

"Besides," Jim added, "I just wish there were something we could do for you."

I could see their concern by their pampering. They tried to make me as comfortable as they could, but no one had a clue this would be my last Sunday at home for over a month. Tending to my needs and taking care of me would soon become a normal lifestyle for them.

After a brief rest, we all went back to church for a special evening program. This often included other arts such as drama and dance. We enjoyed all the presentations, but the choir was the main feature of the evening. That's why I couldn't stay home if I wanted to. I direct the choir. It's all a part of my ministry. I love the ministry of music. Worship is the most joyful, meaningful, and fulfilling part of my life...it is my life.

Getting special songs ready for this took a lot of work, but our choir had rehearsed and was ready. They had several opportunities to share their music with the community, and were loved. People appreciated not only the great sound of the choir, but the contagious spirit of joy they exhumed. The Lord's anointing and presence ministered not only in our presentations, but His Spirit moved powerfully during our rehearsals.

At our last choir practice, a welcomed surprise happened. We could hardly sing...only worship, cry, and pray for each other. I mentioned to them I had some physical problems, and I needed a touch from God. They prayed specifically for the Lord to heal my body supernaturally, or reveal to the doctors the cause so treatment could begin.

As they began to pray collectively and bring my needs before God, I realized these wonderful people would be a major instrument. They would help supply the strength I needed to get through this horrible experience. After feeling weary, I sat down on the front pew. Choir members gathered, and sat at my feet for the longest time.

I sat there, totally exhausted. In my weakness, I could have slumped off the pew and onto the floor prostrate. Yet, I clung to the faith I felt at that moment. I know incredible and amazing things can happen in the presence of the Lord. He inhabits the praise of His people. My expectations soared. The explosive and contagious nature of the heavenly atmosphere created that night began to spread. From the beginning of rehearsal to the end of the evening, everyone's soul and spirit were fed. People began to encourage one another, sharing their innermost thoughts, feelings, and desires.

To see grown men weep, and open themselves up to be so vulnerable in the company of others humbled all of us. Moldable and pliable, we gave way to the sweet presence of our Holy God. Peace and strength returned to my spirit. The feeling of security returned.

We tried to resume practice, but God had different plans. His blessings fell all around us. He communed with His children, meeting their needs. He's such a good God. We rested in His presence, soaking up every glorious minute.

Sunday night the choir sounded amazing. As they sang, God's Spirit moved in a mighty way. His presence and Glory consumed the sanctuary and everyone present.

Every word of this chorus written by Kurt Carr, flowed with anointing and blessings from the Lord. Voices rang out together, "For every mountain You brought me over, for every trial You've seen me through, for every blessing, hallelujah, for this I give you praise!"

Captured by the presence of God, and mesmerized by the emotional display of the choir (lifted hands, tears, and even kneeling) every soul was inspired to worship. We sang the chorus for the last time, and sincere adoration filled our hearts.

The lyrics moved me as I began to break down these words to fit my own circumstances. Yes, this was a huge mountain I thought I'd never be able to climb. The trial I faced seemed so lonely. How did others manage to go through their pain or fears? Yet, I know how blessed I was to have gotten this far without the answers I desperately needed, so I still had to cry, "I give You thanks!"

Praise continued that night. The uncomfortable feeling I had faded in His Glory. My spirit found comfort in His presence. Who is like the Lord?

Exodus 15:11

Who is like unto thee, O Lord, among the gods? Who is like thee, glorious in holiness? fearful in praises, doing wonders?

Unfortunately, reality had to show up and burst the angelic, supernatural bubble surrounding me. By the end of the service, with the odds beating against my faith, I could no longer mask the pain and slowly bent down to sit and rest. The love of Christ I felt through my brothers and sisters in the Lord once again strengthened my faith and encouraged my spirit. I left the service weak, but found comfort in their prayers, hugs, and demonstrations of love. *I felt weak as I left the service ?*

When I got home, I realized the fever had returned. Grateful I didn't have to go to work on Monday, I stayed in bed the next morning. Jim's alarm went off at three o'clock. He made sure I had everything I needed before he left for work. He had been so patient and loving during the last three weeks, and took good care of me. He came home every day at lunch break to fix me something to eat, fluff my pillows, and pamper me. What a prince. *on his ?*

We had always been blessed with good health. Unknown to us, my health problems would be a test of our love, loyalty, and devotion. Soon to go through our worst crisis ever, we didn't realize the vows we took so many years ago would be so severely tested.

After Jim went back to work in the afternoon, I noticed a large, swollen vein protruding from the top of my thigh. It felt firm and warm to the touch. Those symptoms were similar to a blood clot. I panicked and called the doctors' office immediately.

Again, they were hesitant to respond to my cry for help. Their reaction didn't surprise me. I could hear the receptionist sigh, tired of hearing from me day after day. I explained the new development in my condition, and my concerns about a blood clot.

The roller coaster of emotions I had experienced throughout the last three weeks caught up to me. Now, choking back tears, and with a trembling voice, I spoke these words to her, "Call me back—if anyone cares."

"Aw, you really don't mean that do you?" she responded.

I don't know if that was a sincere answer or not. I only knew time would tell the truth. I never did receive a call back from the office that day.

Things felt so hopeless for me. Negative thoughts pounded my consciousness, trying to drive out the inspiration and faith from the previous night. Oh God, this is pathetic. Why can't I get anyone to help me? I don't mean anything to these people.

Disgusted, disappointed, and discouraged, I slipped back down under the paisley printed comforter I had on my bed. I wanted to escape the harsh, cruel reality of an uncompassionate world.

I wanted to pretend, even if for one day, that everything was as it had been a mere three weeks ago. Ignore it and maybe it will go away? I stayed in bed the entire day and into the night, tossing and turning as my temperature spiked even higher.

Monday ran into Tuesday. It was time to get up for work. I struggled and agonized to pull the tight, uncomfortable stockings up my thighs, making me late for work again. Swelling didn't diminish at all. The vein budging at the top of my thigh had worsened. I brought my thermometer to work to monitor the fever during the day.

Because of the holiday, we were short on staff at the Veterinary Hospital. Answering phones, releasing our furry friend patients, and dispensing medications kept us on our toes. There was no option for me to leave any earlier. So, at lunchtime I called the clinic to let them know I would be there at the end of my shift...with or without an appointment.

I didn't know how I would make it through the next few hours. My co-workers knew about my condition, and assisted me whenever possible. They tried to comfort me with their words, and show sympathy with a passing smile or encouraging word.

In addition to the swollen, stretched skin of my legs, I had to deal with the stockings. They compressed my feet and ankles, and the top of my thighs. They were extremely hot and horribly tight, but I didn't dare take them off for fear I wouldn't be able to stand or walk. Every time I sat down I wrenched to feel the pull and pinching at the top of the hose. The pressure squeezed so tightly around my thighs I thought I could explode at any moment. The thermometer reading stayed at one hundred two, yet no medicines I took helped bring it down.

Someone finally came in to work an hour early so I could leave. Grateful for any break at all, I thanked everyone and went straight to the clinic. From where I worked, it was right around the corner.

The nurse led me back to a room soon after I arrived. Both my blood pressure and temperature were elevated. I didn't have time to fear what was in the future, for the present consumed my mind. I just had to get those stockings off as soon as possible.

I began to peel and pull back the stockings as slow as I could, not to brush the already stretched, swollen skin. I rolled the hose down inch by inch, revealing a red, bulging mass on my thigh. As snug as they were, I don't know how I ever got them pulled up over my knees.

Dr. Simpson had not returned from vacation. Dr. Read was still his replacement. A cool wave of relief rolled over me to see her sweet face appear at the door.

She reacted with surprise when she noticed the shocking difference in my legs since the last time she had seen me just two days ago. Her gaze even startled me. That old familiar spirit found a crack in my faith. Fear began to hover over me, like a dark, cold shadow. She discerned my tension, as she put her hand on my shoulder.

She softly broke the silence with her voice, "There is something definitely wrong here, and we're going to find out what it is." She paused for a moment before she asked, "Are you okay?"

The warm compassion I heard in her voice helped cut through the anxiety and tension.

"I don't know," I cried, not being able to hold back the tears. "I can't do this anymore."

Once again, reassuring me with a gentle touch, she said, "I'm so sorry you're going through this, but I'm sending you to the hospital. I'll order a CAT scan and other tests. We will find out what's going on."

The tears wouldn't stop, but I tried to gain my composure to thank her.

"You'll be fine, so try not to worry," she added.

I finally managed to stop crying to tell her, "Dr. Read, I want you to know my family and friends have been praying for me, and that makes a world of difference."

"Oh yes, I believe it. You'll be in my prayers, too. Please stay in touch with me. I'll be checking to see what they find out at the hospital. God bless."

I was comforted to know she believed in the power of prayer. Everyone had been asking the Lord to reveal the cause of this condition. This was confirmation for me. I only had to rest in the security of knowing He cares, and will work things out on my behalf. It's a promise He's given to His people.

*This is the 1st mention of where you work, although you talked about work on page 3.

3 THE DIAGNOSIS

My family, my history, and my heritage all played an important part in my survival. Had I not been grounded in faith, along with having the support of loved ones around me, I couldn't have survived this dreadful experience. Three long weeks of suffering, waiting and wondering had passed. Finally, the time came to find the underlying cause of my condition.

We arrived at the hospital around 5:30 in the evening. Check-in procedures are always time consuming. The nurses took my vitals. Both temperature and blood pressure were elevated and at dangerous levels. From there, they took me back to another large room. Many other patients awaited treatment.

Hours passed, and so did the people coming through the Emergency Room. This place exposed the part of life nobody wants to see or remember. Pain, accidents, heart attacks, injuries and death become too real and tangible. The rawness and unfairness of this experience will stay in my mind forever. No one next to me died during the night, thank God. I saw and heard many things that left my spirit heavy and burdened.

A woman next to me had been restrained to her bed. Drugs played games with her mind as she mumbled continuously, calling out names, profanities, and begging to be loosed from the straps that constrained her. Nothing she said made any sense. I couldn't imagine this being her daily behavior. She cried out for a cigarette to calm her nerves, and continued to shout obscenities when no one responded.

Someone else on the other side of me had been in a car accident, crying out because of the pain. I prayed quietly for her. My discomfort paled in the face of her excruciating trauma. Other patients had similar immediate problems, requiring immediate treatment.

As my sweet husband drifted in and out of sleep, I wondered if they'd forgotten me. After an hour, nurses and medical staff came to talk to me and ask hundreds of questions. Blood work started. It was the first of many repetitive tests.

"Oh, just a little stick," they'd tell me.

"Yeah, right," I thought to myself, and began to mock them every time they came to get more. The nurses laughed, but continued to fill tube after tube with my precious blood, not knowing I was anemic and needed every ounce I had.

Lying on a one-inch slab of cold, plastic foam covered with a rough, white sheet, my swollen left leg throbbed with every beat of my heart. I couldn't find a comfortable position. As my condition grew worse, desperation set in. Surely, they had to find an answer soon.

A team of interns came to question me again. They always came in groups of two or more. Their job was to interrogate me, and discuss the case with each other. This particular medical center is known to be a learning facility. I felt like their guinea pig, or personal experiment.

A few hours passed when I finally saw a real doctor, only to find the chest x-ray taken earlier showed nothing. A Computerized Axial Tomography (CAT) scan was ordered, but the techs had already left for the night. I had to wait for someone to come back in to the hospital to administer the test. This whole process made a long night.

A cloud of depression continued to hover over the ER. It darkened the atmosphere and crushed any evidence of hope. The man next to me moaned with unbelief as the doctor tried to explain another dismal diagnosis. The little boy across the room clung to his mother. I could hear the trembling, anxiety and fear in his voice. There were so many who seemed worse off than me. It prompted me to pray more earnestly. After all, I had the comfort of my Savior and the support of my devoted husband to hold onto.

I glanced at Jim. He was trying to stay cognizant and alert for my sake, but I watched as his eyelids got heavier. Soon, his head dropped to his chest, quickly jolting him from drifting off into sleep. He was up early for work and hadn't eaten since noon. Few and brief naps were inevitable; yet they didn't come easy given the situation. Maybe our minds could have been occupied with television, but there were none in the ER.

Noticing how uncomfortable Jim looked sitting on an awkward stool beside my bed, a considerate young aid brought him a chair. It didn't offer him much more comfort, but it had a back to rest on. As he drifted back off to sleep again, I resumed my prayers.

Between the hard bed, bright lights, and noises of the room, I couldn't find rest or comfort anywhere. One nice thing happened when a nurse brought me a wonderful "baked" blanket right out of the microwave, and placed it over my legs. Those acts of kindness helped change the cold, impersonal atmosphere for me. I thanked her. She remembered to cover me again with a fresh, warm blanket before she left her shift.

The blood cultures turned out to be the most unpleasant experience of the evening. To do a culture, a layer of skin had to be scraped off my arm. Because the first hadn't been successful, they had to do the skin scraping again on the other arm. I began to lose patience. I wanted to lash out at her, and shout the first words that came to my mind. That type of behavior would have been hurtful and not Christ-like at all. I had to keep in mind everyone there tried to do his or her best. I had to remain patient.

Jim made all the phone calls necessary to our family and friends. He let them know what happened to me. He told them not to worry, and not to come, but we knew they would. Our Pastors, James and Jilline Bond, arrived to offer encouragement and prayer. Soon after their visit, the technicians showed up to do the CAT scan. Now we could get on with it, do the test, end the drama and find out what's wrong. I could get some meds, and go home!

The young woman with a twisted knee was discharged; the little boy with his mother was sent home, and the woman in the accident was admitted for surgery. I don't know what ever happened to the older woman making nasty blurbs and comments. I could only whisper another prayer for her, and believe the Lord saw her situation and would help her.

Jim and I tried to rest. The doctor finally came back to let us know that the results of the CAT scan were in. It showed my right kidney had a large tumor. I watched Jim's countenance fall to the floor, but it didn't surprise me at all. I thought this tumor might be related to other hereditary problems. ~~One of my sisters~~

My one sister had a large ovarian tumor removed with a hysterectomy. My mother had a large growth on her bladder. They removed it with laser surgery, and she went home the same day. Both of those tumors were benign. My situation would be the same. Maybe it would take a bit more time to remove and recover, but it was no big deal. CANCER? Not a chance. It never crossed my mind.

Then quietly and without any reserve the word cancer slipped through the doctor's lips. She seemed emotionless. Had she gotten so used to delivering this type of diagnosis and forgotten not everyone accepts this term as common? Jim had a blank, almost lost expression on his face, but it didn't affect me or shake me up.

I received the information with a child-like innocence. Similar to my sister and my mother, this condition should end with the same results. The biopsy will be benign and the tumor will be removed, plain and simple.

Nevertheless, I had to be admitted. They had to do further testing, and of course, more blood work. I thanked the doctor, which seemed like a dumb thing to do after someone just delivered such horrible news to you. But what else could I say? I was definitely in denial.

Soon more young doctors in training approached my bedside. I don't think they ever slept. I gave them the nickname "the kids" because of their age. They came to learn, ask questions, poke and prod. Intrigued by their inquisitive young faces, I knew they were there for the education, and experience. I had to appreciate their inspiration to help and to heal. Headed for degrees in the medical field, they pressed on to attain their dreams.

A thought came to me. Doctors spend years to accomplish something that God can perform in a moment, in a breath, with a Word or thought. The medical profession still won't ever have all the answers. In years to come, they will still be practicing. Through God's mercy, he has granted mankind ~~with~~ a wealth of information, revelation, and understanding to do just that; find a way to heal and mend people.

Most of these interns seemed quiet and reserved. They had to pry and invade my privacy. I am sure they felt awkward asking so many questions. The extra output on my part disturbed me at first. Each time they came I had to explain everything, all my symptoms, pains, when did it start, and how did I feel? When the licensed doctor arrived, he asked the same questions. I'd give the same answers. I tried to help the young doctors as much as I could. To learn their craft, they needed this time and experience.

After speaking to them, they assured me the magnetic resonance imaging (MRI) would show more details, but I had to stay in the hospital until all tests were completed and concrete information had been gathered. They promised a room would be assigned to me where I could finally get some rest. After lying on this hard bed for almost twenty- four hours, my patience had worn thin.

Around three o'clock in the morning, I dragged myself out of bed and hobbled to the nurse's station to remind them I needed a room. I, not so graciously, instructed the staff to do something soon or I would put my clothes back on, leave this place and get a hotel room down the street until they were ready for me. The nurses just laughed, but forty-five minutes later plans were confirmed to move me into a room, and leave the ER, after being there twenty-four hours.

Disgusted and tired, I only had pessimistic thoughts to entertain me. I didn't dare imagine what Jim had been pondering. I am an encourager at heart, but found no words to comfort him now.

I knew one of his concerns would be missing work. The plant Jim worked for allowed no compensation for times like these. We didn't have an emergency fund to fall back on. Production was slow. In his heart though, regardless of loss of time, or money, he stood right by my side. The Lord saw us through financial hardship before. We couldn't stop trusting Him now. He's never let us down. His word declares this promise to always provide for our needs.

Psalm 37:25

...yet have I not seen the righteous forsaken,
nor his seed begging bread.

As he tossed and turned trying to find a comfortable spot, I sensed his reservations. We had never gone through anything like this before, but our love was strong. Even when our love runs out, God's perfect love steps in to fill the gap. In the past when Jim and I failed each other, God's love and compassion yielded strength and inspiration. We've never been left alone. We depended on His grace to carry us through.

2 Corinthians 12:9

And he said unto me, my grace is sufficient for thee: for my strength is made perfect in weakness. Most gladly therefore will I rather glory in my infirmities, that the power of Christ may rest upon me.

Finally transferred to my room, I cringed to think of nurses waking me up all through the night for blood work, to check vitals, or administer medications. Unfortunately, as soon as I arrived, this routine continued.

It was a relief, however, to be discharged from the cold, crowded, and noisy ER. The chair next to my hospital bed seemed a slight improvement for Jim. He expected to get some real rest. I had accepted the idea of staying there for a while. The sun had gone down and come back up during our ordeal. We were both exhausted and wiped out. I begged Jim to go home and get some rest.

"Jim, please go home, or get a bite to eat or something. You're so tired and you need rest."

"I don't want to leave you," he responded faintly.

That's one of the things I love about him. When it came to our relationship, he always showed concern and sensitivity. Hesitantly and slowly rising from his chair, he came and stood at the other side of my bed. He looked half asleep.

I tried to reassure him, "Honey, everything's going to be okay. I'll try to get some rest too. Yeah, fat chance if they let me. Anyway, there shouldn't be any more tests until this afternoon or tomorrow. I doubt the doctor will be in before then."

He stared at me for a minute, as if he would never see me again. Just then, looking into his eyes, it hit me. Until that moment, I hadn't really considered how life threatening my condition could be. I hadn't taken any of the findings seriously. What if the doctors were right? What if it was cancer and Jim's fears were real? In that instant I realized I had to be strong for him, but how could I? With tears welling up in my eyes, I mustered the strength to speak.

"Everything will be fine," I whispered, trying to convince myself at the same time. It was hard for me to believe it, let alone encourage my best friend.

"I'm not going anywhere," I continued. "It'll be okay, and I'll still be here when you get back. At least get something to eat, check the house, and I'll see you this afternoon. I love you."

He agreed, "Alright, but call me if you need me for anything, anything at all. I'm only going to shower and change. I'll be right back."

He stretched his strong arms out, and covered me like a big mother hen. I felt like a little baby bird safely nested under the warmth and safety of her mother's wings. I didn't want him to remove his comforting arms. I felt so secure with him there. Everything within me wanted him to stay.

"I love you Jim," I said as I began to tremble.

"I love you too," he whispered, as we stared into each other's eyes.

"And I won't lose you. I can't, I just can't," he continued saying as he caressed my fingertips and lifted my forearm to stroke against his face.

In my spirit, I struggled to let him go. I needed him. Jim was my rock, my anchor, and my best friend. I took one last deep breath and somewhere found the courage to exhale a few words to convince him to leave.

"Please go. No more tears now. We will get through this together. But you can't help me if you're not strong, so go. Get something to eat. Get some rest. We'll face whatever comes next. I'll try to get some rest too."

Still staring at each other, Jim stood up. Gradually, I felt our fingertips begin to part. We both worked up a smile as he started toward the door. With our eyes still engaged, he blew me a kiss and disappeared around the corner.

4 I BELIEVE IN MIRACLES

I needed a miracle. I still believe in miracles, because I personally know of several which happened in my lifetime. Sometimes it can happen in an instant. Other times miracles can be a result of much prayer and fasting.

Many years ago, my family participated in church events called a " Shut In". I treasure the experiences I received from these special gatherings, which helped shape and cultivate my spiritual life. Learning the importance of prayer, as well as the powerful key of fasting, enriched my walk with God. In those times, real spirituality was birthed in my soul.

As a church family, we would fast Friday, Saturday, and part of Sunday. That means we sacrificed eating to focus on the things of the Lord. After church on Sunday, the fast was broken with a light meal of soup and crackers.

On Friday, everyone gathered together at the church. Some people had the flexibility to come early on Friday morning. They would read or pray. Most people usually arrived later in the evening after work. To get through the next few days of confinement with God and each other, they brought blankets, pillows, Bibles, Bible games and personal items. For the entire weekend we sang, received Biblical teaching, and inspirational instruction. We prayed corporately for each other and immediate needs.

We posted shifts, and prayer was offered throughout the night. One would think people would have been exhausted, but I've seen those who went hours past the end of their shift to continue praying. This went on through the weekend.

Being a young mother, I had to put in the extra effort to feed three small children. I had no babysitter because most of my family participated in the fast. Our kids stayed at the church with us. Handling children in this type of situation was a real task, but I can't remember any of my kids acting up. Surprisingly, they were very well behaved. Even the smallest child recognized and reverenced the awesome presence of God.

Jim's brother-in-law, Hank, had a sister who came to this special meeting. Brenda had been diagnosed with cervical cancer. Because of the advanced stage of the disease, her doctor estimated she had only six months to live. I can't say we heard an audible voice from heaven that weekend, saw a bolt of lightning or bright, flashing lights, or a special angelic appearance, but after she visited her doctor the following Monday, tests results showed the cancer had shrunk ninety percent.

Wait, why only ninety percent? No one has the answer to that question but God. Doctors had no explanation for this change. Treatment was administered to finish the work and remove the rest of the cancer. There was no doubt in our minds that God's divine hand did an amazing work. I wouldn't trade my experiences for anything. I was blessed to know others who were touched by the Hand of God.

There was a woman in our local church who was diagnosed with cancer also. They found it in her leg and needed to do surgery right away to remove it. By the time the surgeons went in to remove the tumor, it was all neatly dried up and encapsulated in its' own sac. Astonished to see what they found, they removed the sac with no complications. To date, they hadn't seen anything like it. There is no medical explanation for what happened.

Another young woman became critically ill. Her kidney function shut down because there were numerous cancerous tumors all over them. Pastor went to pray for her, and to give her a word of encouragement from the Lord. He told her not to worry for this sickness was not unto death and God had everything under control.

These words were a great confirmation for Lonnie. The night before she had been in contact with a close friend of hers who lived in another state. Her friend's pastor had a dream about Lonnie and had the same message, this sickness was not unto death. This confirmation raised Lonnie's faith, along with the rest of her family. They believed God together. They refused to settle for the grim and hopeless report the doctors gave them. They chose to believe the report of the Lord.

The church prayed, and God answered. New kidneys appeared. To many of the doctors' amazement, the urethra tube, which had not been there since birth, miraculously formed and began to function. She received a miracle. No one could explain it. The evidence of a miracle was found in the tests. Before and after images showed God's healing power for all to see.

Even our dear Pastor Jill received a miraculous healing from the Lord. She was in the hospital for a routine surgery, but something happened during the procedure. The complications caused Jill's entire system to shut down. Her doctors explained nothing could be done and gave her no hope of recovery. Jill needed a divine touch from God to live.

While visiting Jill at the hospital, she began to cry out in pain and desperation. Her mother and I were with her at the time. We held her. We began calling out to God. Only He could heal and deliver her. As we began to intercede on her behalf we felt the warm, peaceful presence of God fill the room. The Lord responded and touched Jill's body, delivering her from the fate of death. When our faith grabs hold and touches the heart of God nothing is impossible.

In another testimony, the Lord delivered my nephew Tai in a mighty way. Nearly one and one half years old, he was diagnosed with spinal meningitis. The news devastated the family. The condition reached such a critical state that even if he did live through it, the doctors explained he might lose his hearing and balance. They were confident this young boy would never be a strong, healthy, active child. The fever subsided and the doctors did all they could. Tai could not walk. Thankfully, the disease didn't take his life. They took Tai home.

Once home, he could barely stand for a minute, let alone walk. He continued to bounce off the walls in the hallway falling every time he tried to walk. His parents were content with the small improvement. I reminded Bek and Hank God can heal one hundred percent, and we should pray for total recovery. Tai not only recovered, but grew to be one of the best athletes in our community. Trophies from wrestling, football and baseball line the walls of their home. His hearing returned to normal...except for those few selective moments when he chose not to listen!

No medical explanations can be given for each of these accounts, but they are all true and documented. What I don't understand is why these amazing stories remain hidden from the public? The wonderful testimonies of miracles get tucked away in medical journals somewhere, like there is a conspiracy to hide the marvels of God. These miracles are the very evidence of His handiwork.

I've witnessed these things God did for others. Because of these great testimonies my faith stayed strong through the darkness of my personal crisis. I knew too much about what our Mighty God can do. I couldn't begin to doubt Him. He can do anything. He's more than able to answer our prayers.

Ephesians 3:20,21

Now unto him that is able to do exceeding abundantly above all that we ask or think, according to the power that worketh in us, Unto him be glory in the church by Christ Jesus throughout all ages, world without end, Amen.

Since the creation of the world, God has been performing miracles.

Genesis 1:1, 2

In the beginning God created the heaven and the earth. And the earth was without form, and void, and darkness was upon the face of the deep. And the spirit of God moved upon the face of the waters.

It's hard to comprehend how the Lord can create something out of nothing. When you read the book of Genesis in the Bible, the whole creative process is miraculous to say the least. Who can understand the mighty omniscient, omnipresent, and supernatural power of God?

God created us and loved us from before eternity. He has a plan for each of our lives. He knows exactly how to use these events and experiences to develop faith and character.

He has a plan for me. I see it more clearly each day as my life unfolds. Why does God choose a different approach for every situation? I don't have the answer, but I do know I saw Him heal and deliver. Whether it's in an instant, a brief moment, or through the process of time, God has a purpose. God has a plan here.

5 AN ANSWER TO PRAYER

Despite the present dark valley I found myself in, the Lord answered prayers daily. Even though exhaustion tried to dampen any sign of faith left in my soul, the dimmer the situation, the more light I saw from His blessings and joy. Life-giving scriptures swept through my mind along with hundreds of inspirational songs. They locked themselves into every corner of my heart, waiting for the moment of release, to burst into my mouth and engage my throat into singing. One particular song, "Your Multiple Mercies", brought a wonderfully encouraging passage to mind:

Lamentations 3:22-24

It is of the Lord's mercies that we are not consumed, because his compassions fail not. They are new every morning: great is thy faithfulness. The Lord is my portion, saith my soul; therefore will I hope in him.

I should have expected the Lord's faithfulness to be the greatest during my most difficult struggle. Today, my first day admitted to the hospital proved to be that day. God answered a very special prayer, resolving and closing a disheartened, painful chapter in my life.

Our oldest daughter, Cheri, was estranged from Jim and me for eight months. Born in November of 1974, Cheri, our first of three children, proved to be such a blessing. Though her strong-willed character created many trying times for us, her generous gift of compassion and love for children was awesome and inspiring.

Married at the age of 19, Cheri's dream became reality when she and husband, Mark, had their own family complete with two beautiful little girls. Makayla was born in November of 1996 (three months after the death of my beloved mother). Jazmine followed a few years later in January of 2000. Life for Cheri didn't turn out to be the dream she hoped for.

She went through a long, dismal period. She strayed from her walk with God. The pressure and stress of working a full-time job, attending evening school, raising two small children, and maintaining a household and marriage wore her down and broke her spirit. She became physically worn and emotionally defeated. Hurt and confused with her marriage falling apart, she packed a few personal belongings and walked out. She not only left her husband, but she left behind her two precious baby girls. Makayla was four, and Jazmine only one and one-half.

Never in a million years would I have guessed my daughter could ever walk away from her own children. They were the reality of her dreams. As a child, Cheri played with baby dolls every day, and pretended to have children of her own. As a youth, she babysat children every chance she had, and practiced nurturing and caring for them. She took pride in honing her skills and reaping experience. As a young woman, she longed for her own family and prayed for it. She made the most serious mistake of her life when she allowed the circumstances surrounding her to crush her spirit. Cheri gave up those dreams when she walked out on her family.

We were all overwhelmed with grief to see Cheri and Mark's lives devastated and torn apart. She was doubtful of any future with her husband and family, and embarked on a three-year journey through depression. Hopeless and uncertain, she drifted further away from her commitment to God. She began walking in her own uncontrollable desires and began to walk in a dark wilderness experience.

Cheri knew the decisions she had made and the new lifestyle she had chosen were in direct disobedience of God's will for her life. This path only led her deeper into a whirlwind of disappointments and failures.

Sin is an offense or action against God. It is also against the people we love, not only destroying our divine relationship with our Creator, but also causing havoc within our families. It tears lives apart. Sin will make you do things you thought you would never do, make you go farther than you want to go, stay longer than you intended, and pay a higher price than you bargained for. We are no strangers to the tragedy sin brings.

God created man to live, not die. The consequence of sin is death. The first sin originated in the book of Genesis with Adam. It all comes down to our will and the choices we make. Without spiritual reconciliation and divine intervention, there is no hope for mankind. God gave man the will to choose between right and wrong. The 'First Adam' failed with his relationship with God. This curse continued through generations.

Romans 5:12

Wherefore, as by one man sin entered into the world and death
by sin; and so death passed upon all men, for that all have sinned…

The way Cheri acted did not reflect the values and attitudes she was raised with. She knew the situation in her life concerned her family, and the strain between us became intense. I found myself in a state of depression; sitting in the dark for hours, trying to figure out what I had done wrong in raising this child. I know that's something every parent goes through while searching for answers.

For nine months, Cheri alienated herself from her family. Her parents, her sister, Dani, and her brother, Aaron, only felt her indifference instead of the love and affection she once shared with us. She became unreceptive to good or wise instruction, and wouldn't receive any truth spoken into her life.

With only a few short weeks from completing her degree in cosmetology, her continued absence from class caused her to be dismissed from school. Cheri also struggled with keeping a job. The only occasional contact she had with her brother and sister was to borrow money, only to abuse their trust and generosity.

All of Cheri's family and friends did understand her circumstances. We took every opportunity to reach out to her with sympathy and compassion. Everyone prayed for her. Together we held onto God's promise of deliverance. We watched as the Lord kept extending grace and mercy to her, despite her circumstances.

She had an apartment located in a section of town where there was several shootings and robberies. One of the men she lived with struggled with drug addiction and anger issues. He put his fist through the bedroom wall during a heated argument. Yet God's umbrella of protection covered her and kept her from danger.

We all knew, more important than anything, Cheri loved her family. Nothing would ever prevail against the strong ties we had together. Certainly, once she found out about my terrible diagnosis nothing could stop her from coming to me.

Jim hadn't been gone long, and returned to the hospital to be with me. I slept only a little, but felt peaceful the moment he stepped in the door. We only had a few moments together before we saw our first visitor appear in the hallway. I will never forget the look on her face as she slowly entered the room. The long night in the ER left me weak. I still felt the shock of receiving the diagnosis of cancer. That combination along with the emotion of seeing Cheri for the first time in eight months overwhelmed me.

When I saw her approach the doorway of my room, I couldn't catch my breath. Even though I expected to see her at some point, I froze. In the silence of the moment I could hear my heart beat. We waited for this day, although never expecting the circumstances surrounding this meeting to be so life threatening.

Cheri's eyes, filled with pools of water, never glanced my way. Focused on her daddy, she stumbled across the room falling into Jim's arms. My mind flashed back to see how she once ran to him for comfort after falling off her bicycle. This was one of those priceless moments, when only in her daddy's arms could she find relief from her brokenness. Time stopped in space as I watched them embrace and weep together. It was a dream Jim and I had been longing and praying for.

Tears, now streaming down her face, fell like raindrops. On the front of her bright red tee shirt, they made a pattern of irregular, darkened dots.

"She can't have cancer," she whispered to her father in disbelief, and then buried her face deeply in his chest.

"It's okay baby," he replied, trying to calm her. *with her*

We hadn't spoken *for* so long. What could we say to our child to help her? My tongue seemed to be stuck to the back of my throat. I tried to swallow, *to* and lose the choking sensation I felt, but I said the only thing that came to my mind.

"I'll be fine."

Lifting her head, she shouted in desperation, "No! It's my fault! It's all my fault!"

Choked with emotion and surprise, Jim tried to console her, "You didn't do this honey. You had nothing to do with…"

Cutting him off she cried, "Mom has cancer because of me…because of what I did."

She finally turned to look at me. When our eyes met, years of memories flashed across my mind. Oh, how I love my baby girl. I missed her. I too wanted to clutch her, hold her tight, and make all of this go away.

I felt the meltdown coming. My face burned, and my stomach twisted. I had no other choices. I had to ride along with this emotional crisis going on before my eyes.

Before I had the chance to collect my thoughts, she blurted out her greatest fear.

"I know you prayed for God to do whatever it takes to bring me back, and now this!"

The tears kept falling as she declared, "Because of me, because of me you're sick. Oh, I'm so sorry, this can't be happening, I'm so sorry."

She sobbed uncontrollably, and continued to anguish over her confession as her father kept her cradled tightly in his arms.

I fought to keep my composure, and to comfort her.

"No, Cheri," I said, "God wouldn't punish you or me like that. He's not a God of revenge. He's not mad at you. You have to understand, His ways are much higher than ours. He's loving and merciful. This isn't a judgment or type of punishment."

I then repeated insistently, "He's not mad at you."

She still hadn't made any motion to come over to me, probably because of the comfort and security she felt nestled in her daddy's arms. I found it difficult to muster any other words to encourage her.

It was true. I did pray for the Lord to do whatever it took to get my daughter back. I had been desperate for her to return to the Lord and be reconciled with her husband and children. I never considered the consequences of saying that prayer, but I don't regret it. This had to be the answer. Only the Lord can use a situation like this and turn it around to benefit all those who are involved.

Romans 8:28

And we know that all things work
together for good to them that love God…

I knew that scripture very well. I can't number the times I have quoted this verse during difficult times that just didn't make sense. I believed it with all my heart, and was willing to accept those terms because it was all for our good.

6 I NEED MY FAMILY

My family has always been a very close-knit unit. I had a great life growing up in Milton, a small community in Northeastern Pennsylvania. My parents, Ed and Jean Hoch, helped me create so many wonderful memories. Cindy, the older of two sisters, was followed by Cathy ten months later. Because I arrived seven years later, I often teased mom and wondered if they had planned my birth.

Our home sat across from Lincoln Street Park. I had my own playground complete with swings, monkey bars, a huge sliding board, seesaws, and a king-size merry-go-round. The park also had the biggest, most wonderful sandbox I'd ever seen. With plenty of friends and loads of imagination, I kept busy and out of trouble.

Our parents planned a vacation every year to the beach, or maybe fishing in Canada. I needed nothing. Mr. and Mrs. Hoch successfully established a good name for our family in the small community we lived in. We were never considered rich, but in those days material possessions didn't seem to matter. You knew if you had food, clothing and shelter, and two nickels to rub together, you were extremely blessed and happy.

As I remember, a nickel was all you needed to buy a double-dip, chocolate fudge ice cream cone. None of my friends got allowances. If you wanted anything extra you would get a part-time job. Teens never drove the family car either. You bought a car when you were old enough. You paid for your own expenses including gas and car insurance. We were taught good principles and ethics. My father was a man of his word and a man of integrity. He passed on good habits of discipline to the rest of the family. This must have come from being in the military for the better part of his life.

Dad's way of doing things left a little craving in my personality to be a perfectionist. I never considered myself dysfunctional though. We had a very functional family. Our family was very typical for that time period in the sixties. I started school at the tender age of five. I walked to school every day. Not only did I walk to school in the morning, but also came home to eat lunch, and then back for the afternoon.

From time to time I still get together with the girlfriends I went to school with. Five of us were born in January. We love to reminisce about the good old days. We have remained friends throughout the years. During my fight with cancer, those friends came, lifted my spirits with laughter, and stirred up happy and precious memories. It's wonderful we've been together for so long.

My mother held a part-time job outside the home. I hold dear the memories of coming home after school to smell the aroma of a home-cooked meal. The fragrance of furniture polish filled the air. She loved to keep the house tidy and clean. You could always hear pleasant music when you walked in the door. We had an old stereo/record player in the living room she loved to play her records on.

Holidays were a wonderful treat because she decorated the house special for every occasion. Easter was filled with flowers, decorated eggs, and the pastel colors of spring. Many picnics were planned for summertime with all of the regular fixings. We had hot dogs and hamburgers on the grill. We enjoyed plenty of pickled eggs, potato salad, with home-made ice cream and cake.

Autumn, with its natural vibrant colors, filled the whole house as well as the back yard. The mountains in Pennsylvania were picturesque this time of year. Christmas was our favorite holiday. The house overflowed with the smell of homemade Christmas cookies. Greens and lights adorned the windows. Wonderful music filled the air.

Mom's constant humming always left me feeling comforted and secure. Every day she had a smile to share. She never spoke a harsh word about anybody. Mom had a heart of compassion and a sensitive nature that made you feel glad to be home. There's no place like home. She certainly made it a castle for our family. I felt so proud if someone told me I was just like her. The dreams I carried as a child were simple. I just wanted to be like my mother and raise a family of my own. I welcomed the day I could love someone, and take care of him the way mom took care us.

My dream came true in August of nineteen seventy when I met a young man. His name was James Ward. We married three years later, and our lives became very hectic. It wasn't until after our first baby was born God gently tugged on our hearts. We wanted to raise our children in church. They needed to know everything about the Lord and His saving grace. We were ready to obey God's voice. When we thought our child was the one who needed Christ, it was really our hunger leading us back to Him.

We then decided to join the few faithful members at Christ Temple, his father's church. I attended church all of my life, but this was where I found a personal, and intimate relationship with the Lord. As a child, I learned all the Bible stories. I even memorized the books of the Bible, but never grasped the concept of a true relationship with Him.

I recall the beautiful stained-glass windows, the mastery of architecture covering the pillars and archways of that historic building. I went every Sunday, yet something was missing. My concept of Jesus included a special child, whose mother's name was Mary. They were so poor his crib was a manger. He grew up to be a carpenter, and died a cruel death on a cross. Somewhere in between Sunday school, Vacation Bible School, and Catechism Class, I missed the true meaning of salvation. I don't ever remember being taught about a new birth:

John Chapter 3:3-7

Jesus answered and said unto him, Verily, verily, I ay unto thee, Except a man be born again, he cannot see the kingdom of God. Nicodemus saith unto him, How can a man be born when he is old? can he enter the second time into his mother's womb, and be born? Jesus answered, Verily, verily I say unto thee, Except a man be born of water and of the Spirit, he cannot enter into the kingdom of God. That which is born of the flesh is flesh; and that which is born of the spirit is spirit. Marvel not that I said unto thee, Ye must be born again.

When Christ used the term verily, verily in this text, He wanted people to pay attention and listen. You must be born again, or you cannot enter into the kingdom of God. This is pretty important information. Also, I didn't know the powerful acts of healing and deliverance spoken about in the Bible could actually happen today. The acts, wonders, and demonstrations of power the Apostles had were overlooked and not a part of the present-day church.

At that time, a powerful and awesome wonder became reality to me. I heard about Jesus, and how He's a wonderful Savior. As a member of Christ Temple, the worship and level of spiritual living I saw was totally different from what I experienced. There were no stained-glass windows, but the light found there was incredible. There were no marvelous works of carpentry, but the old wooden floors swayed with the beat of the music. You could almost feel the heartbeat of God. No glorious archways were present in this small chapel, but when you entered the door to the sanctuary you felt something powerful, something divine. There, in that little one room chapel with old wooden floors and a beautiful hand-made wooden baptistery, I discovered forgiveness, remission for my sins, and righteousness, peace, and joy in the Holy Ghost.

Romans 14:17

*For the kingdom of God is not meat and drink;
but righteousness, and peace, and joy in the Holy Ghost.*

I received the born again experience Christ mentioned in the Bible. Since the day I met the Lord, I discovered His mercies are new every morning with each brand-new day. For every mountain He's brought me over, for every trial He's seen me through, for every blessing, Hallelujah! For this I give Him praise! I made a commitment to God to live for Him.

We were both hungry for God, and began to learn more and more about Jesus. Jim's older Brother, Archie, kept things operating smoothly at the church. He was a tremendous Bible teacher. I would sit in awe of the simplicity of his teaching. Yet, Archie could dig into the deeper things of God and make you hungry for more. This is a true gift of God.

Jim's mother, Lucille, became an inspiration to me. I had many questions, and called her often during the week. She never minded giving me guidance and helped me understand the scriptures I couldn't interpret by myself. I wanted more of Jesus and I believe what I was taught in those days lay the foundation for my strength and faith today. The Word has brought me through many situations. I remember a time when the spirit of fear was very strong in my life. Fear happens to be one of the greatest hindrances to God's people, but it doesn't have to be.

2nd Timothy 1:7

For God hath not given us the spirit of fear;
but of power, and of love, and of a sound mind.

I wrote that scripture on small, colorful pieces of notepaper and placed them in several rooms of my home. I read it every day out loud. I repeated this exercise several times a day for as long as it took for the Word to penetrate my spirit, build my faith, and remove the fear plaguing my mind. I discovered how powerful His word really was. I now know how to get rid of fear. It is so important to hide God's Word deep in our hearts.

Psalm 119:11

Thy word have I hid in mine heart, that I might not sin against thee.

His Word is the final authority. I've used this experience throughout my life to overcome many obstacles, stumbling blocks, and narrow tunnels. The more of His word I learn, the more power I have to overcome.

In our early days at Christ Temple there were just a handful of young people. Jim's Sister, Rebekah, was a greatly anointed singer, song leader, and recording artist. She received a calling from the Lord at an early age, and was a faithful servant. Because of her obedience to the work of God, He used her ministry to bless and inspire others.

After Jim and I began attending church, Rebekah decided to revive a small choir. I sat in wonder as those few young people gathered around the old antique upright piano and lifted their voices together. I remembered myself as a child singing songs out of the church hymnbook. These young people sang old, spiritual choruses that were not familiar to me. Nevertheless, I loved this inspiring, joyful experience. The love, unity, and oneness I felt from the spirit of my newfound family became overwhelming. Soon, the songs they sang echoed in my heart continually. I felt His spirit moving so deeply in a part of my soul I didn't know existed. It left me feeling whole and complete.

I discovered how to praise the Lord as we sang, "Oh how marvelous, how wonderful, and my song shall ever be, Oh how marvelous, how wonderful, is my Savior's love for me" and, "Oh, how I love Jesus". Every day I sang those songs. I never heard gospel music before. I didn't know Christian music existed outside of the religious tunes from my past. It got a grip on me right away. Not just the music, but also the message of faith as well.

The words of Gospel music can minister to the very depths of a person's soul. God's Word delivered through the vehicle of music travels through the emotions of man. It fills the emptiness and longing of the heart, mind and soul. Everyone has an empty place that longs for God. This is the empty place that desires to know Him. Our spirit responds to His Word and His Word will set you free. The power of gospel music can change and deliver you.

I Samuel 16:23

"And it came to pass, when the evil spirit from God was upon Saul, that David took an harp, and played with his hand; so Saul was refreshed, and was well, and the evil spirit departed from him."

What a supernatural event! It's so powerful to know through music God can deliver us. Music has always been a part of my life, but never has it had an effect on me like gospel music. I enjoyed this new experience of singing and worshiping with other young people. I found so much purpose in my life being a part of this team. I enjoyed being a part of something so exciting and real. The power and glory of the Lord was revealed to me. It was awesome!

As time went by, I realized the members of this small choir were beginning their journey into adulthood. Because it was difficult to work around job situations, some felt pressured. They juggled, dividing their time between rehearsals, Bible Study, and church events. Some got married and began their families. The number of choir members dwindled until four were left, Jim, Rebekah, her husband Hank, and myself. We continued the ministry as a quartet. This birthed our family ministry.

The Lord opened doors and we walked through them. Our families enjoyed this special closeness God gave us. He blessed us with joy, and the experience of growing in Christ together. We traveled more, singing and ministering at local churches and events.

Our programs included all styles of gospel music. This consisted of Southern and Traditional, Contemporary Christian, and Black Gospel. Our style included solos, duets, trios, and quartets singing. Keeping up with traveling on the weekends and working full-time jobs put a strain on us all. The Lord said, when we are weak, He'd be strong. There is nothing we cannot do through Him.

Philippians 4:13

"I can do all things through Christ which strengtheneth me."

We would squeeze all our equipment and the kids into our car and Bek's. Sometimes it would be a bit uncomfortable, but no one complained. At this point, Jim and I had three children. Our first little girl made her singing debut when she was just three years old. She sang, "Have faith in God." She'd sing it all day long, and mastered a slow vibrato. I remember how proud she looked the day she presented her solo before our little home assembly. Singing loud and strong, she performed with confidence and boldness. Her face lit up with pride, being able to offer her own talent unto the Lord. Cheri would lead the way for the other children in our lives.

Our second daughter, Danielle, was born over two years later. As soon as she could hold a microphone, she started singing. Our most precious memory of her happened after she turned four. We were performing outdoors at a local festival. It happened to be a warm, beautiful Indian summer day in Pennsylvania. Nevertheless, she seemed a bit uncomfortable. This hadn't been her first appearance, but it certainly was the largest group she ever sang in front of. In the middle of her performance she became bothered by an untimely itch. Unfortunately, she was oblivious to the fact she was lifting her dress during her song to get to it! The audience roared with laughter at such innocence. She completed her song without one mistake.

Seventeen months after Danielle was born, we had our son, Aaron. Surrounded by music all his life, he decided very early in life he would not be left out. At only sixteen months old, he snatched the microphone from my hand during a New Years Eve service. He proceeded to cover it with his mouth and bellowed (and drooled), "HAL-LE-YU-LA!!" He was attempting to sing the chorus, "Hallelujah," and the congregation laughed, and applauded with admiration and adoration.

As parents we treasure these delightful moments. We've given our children to Him. We can always trust Him to take care of them when we can't. Be assured if we raise a child to love the Lord, he will never depart from that teaching.

Proverbs 22: 6

Train up a child in the way he should go:
and when he is old, he will not depart from it.

The children were always a part of our ministry. They participated in almost all our programs. They especially loved the Sunday school programs our ministry would deliver to the many churches we were invited to. *where ?* They would sing while Jim's sister, Bek, accompanied them on the piano. She would prepare a children's message for a portion of our program. Being a fifth grade school teacher, she enjoyed gathering the kids and teaching them. Their eyes would dance with glee as she drew them to her side and asked them questions. Often she would sit on the floor with the kids from the congregation and invite them to participate in the brief lesson. People love to hear children sing.

The kids at every church we ministered to loved to be part of the singing and the lesson no matter what age they were. Our own children glowed with pride, sitting among the crowd of smiling faces.

Cheri, Danielle, and Aaron knew they had a very special mission to do for the Lord. They always did their best. For the most part these little disciples were very well behaved. They knew all their songs. They sat on the front pew and sang along with our entire program. The traveling never seemed to bother them or tire them at such young ages. Many times we would leave home before the sun would rise. Their breakfast would be packed and they would usually go back to sleep after being taken from their warm beds. They were real troopers, and would always wake up in time to perform their part, and steal the hearts of the congregation. Other times we would arrive home late on Sunday nights. On a few occasions, I'd let them miss school the following day. They never complained.

I only regret we have no videos or recordings. The only way we have those precious moments stored are in the recesses of our minds. My fondest memory was when my children naturally began to pick up the harmony parts in the songs they sang. Cheri sang soprano, Danielle sang alto, and at the remarkable age of four, Aaron picked up a tenor part. To this day I find it hard to believe, but he heard it, and sang it. They all have that special gift. I stand in awe of the way God created each and every one of us. We were wonderfully created. Each of us came into this world with specific gifts and talents.

James 1:17

Every good gift and every perfect gift is from above, and cometh down from the Father of lights, with whom is no variableness, neither shadow of turning.

All of us were made for a specific reason. We were all designed to fit together like one, large, beautiful picture puzzle. There is a divine purpose for who we are, and why we are here. The Lord has special plans for our lives.

Jeremiah 29:11

For I know the plans I have for you, declares the Lord, plans to prosper you and not to harm you, plans to give you hope and a future. (NIV)

Soon, two more children were added to our ministry. Bek and Hank were blessed with their first child, a son named Tai. This little guy ended up being the jester of the family. We never got him to perform a song with us, but he loved to demonstrate the talent God gave him, which made him quite special. Tai would run out in the aisle of a church to dance and let everyone know he was the main show.

This special child became a large part of our testimony during the early years of ministry. At eighteen months old, he acquired spinal meningitis and almost died. Because of the large amount of white blood cells in his system, he shouldn't have been conscious by the time we got him to the hospital. Upon diagnosis, we were told Tai would suffer severe brain damage. The affects had already robbed his hearing, balance, and could possibly cause blindness.

We knew the Lord had a great purpose for this boy's life. The healing process came quickly without any reminders or repercussions. Tai grew to be one fine student. Contrary to what doctors said, he also became an amazing athlete. How can we ever forget the goodness and grace of God in our lives?

Two years later a sweet baby girl, Shannon, was added to Bek and Hank's family. She too would join in the fun. Too shy to perform, she would just stand with the other children and hold a microphone. It wasn't long before she realized her microphone didn't have a cord. She didn't waste any time letting us know about it, and afterward discovered the boldness to sing.

Our families had grown. Our cars were definitely getting crowded. Jim and I bought a conversion van. We'd all pile in and travel along the eastern coast. Shannon had a little chair that fit nicely between the bucket seats. The other four children were still small enough to fit across the bench in the rear of the vehicle. We packed the equipment and prepared a few sandwiches and snacks. We had the privilege to travel across the country to California, Arizona, and to Barbados. Through that experience alone we realize how blessed we really are. I am so thankful for our many blessings. I appreciate the freedom available in America, this wonderful country.

36

We have so many great memories. Before I realized it, my dreams were coming true. God helped us give our own children the same family structure I knew and treasured. I appreciate the Lord for making it possible. I pray every family would have the opportunity to experience the same closeness.

Unity and wholeness are available to anyone who desires it. Family is the institution created by God from the beginning of time to show His love, and how we are to love one another. He created man and woman to join together and recreate themselves. God wanted the earth to be filled with families loving each other and worshiping Him. It's His desire that everyone be a part of this amazing relationship. Our lives are not complete without Him. He knew we would need a Savior. That's why my life is complete. Not because of who I was, but for who He is in my life.

This chapter about my family is where I came from. Hopefully you will be able to follow this thread through each page and story I've shared, and focus on the message. There were difficult times during those years. As a young mother, I chose to stay home with my children. It was hard to make ends meet. God's Word says the righteous would never be forsaken:

Psalms 37:25:

*I have been young and now am old; yet have I not seen
the righteous forsaken, nor his seed begging bread.*

We stood on that promise, and never went without. God always provided. Yes, we experienced a season when we almost lost everything. Our relationship had been in jeopardy. Our ministry went through a tough transition. Our failures often put us in compromising positions, but we couldn't blame God for the consequences of our foolish actions.

Yet, He is so compassionate, understanding, forgiving and loving. He steps in to gently lead us out of distress. He reconciles our earthly relationships with each other, and brings us back to Him. It's because God so loved the world that He gave His only begotten son.

John 3:16

*For God so loved this world, that he gave his only begotten Son,
that whosoever believeth in him should not perish, but have everlasting life.*

I'm so thankful I know His unconditional love and forgiveness. Sin is what separates a man from God. However, we can be reconciled to God through His redemptive plan. We must first believe He is the Christ that came to deliver us, and the one who died on the cross so we may be saved.

Through reconciliation, we are taken back to our intended purpose and original state. He not only reconciles us back to Him, but in the process heals our relationships. Jesus came so we would have life abundantly.

John 10:10

*....I am come that they might have life, and that
they might have it more abundantly.*

In the next several months my family played a large part in my life, reflecting God's love. Not only my natural family, but also my heavenly family would play their part. Others would see how powerful the unified body of Christ is. One purpose for my illness was evident. The community witnessed the hand of God through my brothers and sisters. We are knit together in a powerfully intimate way. We share the same blood, and identify with each other through the Name of Jesus. I am so glad to be a part of the family of God, and joint heirs with Him.

7 THE POWER OF A TOUCH

The decision was made for me to remain in the hospital until surgery could be scheduled. They were fearful to send me home to wait because of the severe blood clotting and damage to the deep veins in my legs. A surgeon from Neurology would remove the right kidney. A vascular surgeon would be needed to repair the damage in the vena cava. These surgeons had to coordinate their schedules to perform the procedures together. It couldn't be done for at least a week. Now, it was just a matter of time. I had to wait and try to make myself comfortable.

Honestly, I can't say I constantly worried about having cancer. I was probably in a state of denial, but my family had everything to do with my attitude and state of mind. They flooding my time with their presence, prayers, and encouragement. People were eager to express concern, and showed it daily with flowers, gifts, phone calls, and visits. I would be in the hospital for awhile, and had nothing but time on my hands. In the chapter describing my family and ministry, the most important things in my life were my loved ones and my service to God. Being surrounded by family meant the world to me.

I certainly wasn't going to church for a while, so my church came to me. The chapel at the hospital was under construction, so a small office was converted into a temporary sanctuary. Still hooked up with tubes for intravenous fluids and medications, my kids wheeled me downstairs into that small space. No matter what position I found myself in, my legs still ached and throbbed. Nevertheless, as men, women, and children began to pile into that little room, I did my best to hide my discomfort. There were about thirty of us who managed to squeeze into our church service. This was proceeded by singing, thanksgiving, and worship. For us, worship is a form of adoration toward God, as natural as breathing. It's a lifestyle. I felt the Spirit of God immediately, real, thick, and almost tangible.

As part of their praise, my friends chose to sing many of the choir songs I taught them. What a sense of accomplishment, knowing the songs I loved and shared with my church would end up being such a blessing to me. The lyrics meant so much to us. Each line of every song had so much life, and spoke encouragement into my spirit.

They achieved their goal. They teamed together like a regiment of mighty warriors and were on a mission to lift the spirits of their friend. Their presence brought joy, encouragement, and peace. This was just what I needed after being stopped in the middle of life with this crazy detour called cancer.

The service continued with singing, weeping, and reading the Bible. The fellowship was precious. Even the children raised their hands and sang along. They knew the words to every song, and were little ministering angels the Lord sent me. I could see compassion in their fragile, innocent faces. The tender hugs and generous smiles I received meant so much to me.

During our brief service, some read their favorite scriptures, or gave an uplifting testimony. Nobody could complete his or her thoughts without choking up. With trembling voices and teary eyes, they expressed in their own personal ways how much I meant to them. They thanked God for keeping me alive, and offered Him honor, glory, and praise for His goodness toward me. This was a great example of friends and families learning together what living and loving was all about.

This is the love I experienced from family and church family. I saw Jesus in their faces. What wonderful expressions of kindness I received from these people. Never before did I receive so much personal prayer and attention. For one moment in time, everyone's focus was on me. The sense of belonging, being needed, being loved, and feeling so important is truly humbling. It's so powerful to experience the kind of bonding and closeness that takes place through the Spirit of God. This love is strong, undivided and untouchable.

In the Bible, David and Jonathan had the most amazing relationship. It takes a spiritual mind to imagine a relationship between two men so intimate. The Bible says their souls were knit together. What an incredible, amazing description of closeness:

1 Samuel 18:1

And it came to pass, when he had made an end of speaking unto Saul,
That the soul of Jonathan was knit with the soul of David,
and Jonathan loved him as his own soul.

A very special, personal event then came to my mind. God uses ordinary people to love and touch others. A few years ago during a revival service, the Lord used me to bless someone. The spirit was high and so thick you could almost see it. You could feel faith in the air. Jesus stepped into the house just like He was in that little makeshift chapel.

Close to the end of the service, I noticed a young woman seated about half way back in the church. She was worshiping God with all her heart. I felt the Spirit urge me to go and pray with her. She welcomed me with open arms. We stood and prayed together. The Spirit of God took over. I called out to God to accomplish the work He already began in her. I sensed He was working on her behalf, and spoke words of faith to her soul. I didn't know the circumstances in her life, and didn't need to know. God knew.

What concluded was extreme praise! We stood there hugging, weeping, and magnifying God in the beauty of His holiness. I don't know how much time had passed, but we were enjoying this moment of bliss in the Spirit. For that minute there was not a single problem, grief, heartache or pain attached to our lives. We simply bathed in the beauty of His love and in the rivers of God's living waters.

A few months after the service, this young woman wrote a letter to Pastor Bond, stating she had cervical cancer and God healed her the night we prayed together. Bless the Name Of Jesus!! Hallelujah!! Did I do that? Did I obtain a supernatural gift, and heal her from this disease? No, I've never claimed to have the gift of healing, but for whatever reason, God chose me as a vessel on that particular night. He used me as an instrument for His glory. I became an extension of His arm to show forth His amazing grace, mercy and His healing virtue. The memory of that night will be embedded in my mind forever. He needed someone and He used me. Not because I was special, but because God uses ordinary people. When the Lord healed in the Bible, it was usually generated by a touch from the Master, or getting close enough to touch Him in some way.

Matthew 14:36

And besought him that they might only touch the hem of his garment: and as many as touched were made perfectly whole.

I believe in the power of His touch, and how He imparts His gifts through His children. We are an extension of His garment, His body, and His virtue. The story of the young woman reminded me God still heals. Whether He chose to use the world of medicine, or supernaturally through His people, I believed I would not die.

The service at the hospital concluded in that small room, but love lingered. I was tired. My body and legs were achy, but I could have stayed there all day. I needed to soak in the warmth of His presence, bask in His love, and peace. I don't know how anyone can survive in this world without His presence.

The Bible says no man has ever seen the face of God, but the reflection of God in the faces of His people created a wonderful image of what He looks like. I could only be overtaken with courage and believe everything would indeed be all right.

Psalms 23:4

"Yea, though I walk through the valley of the shadow of death, I will fear no evil; for thou art with me; they rod and they staff they comfort me."

connotation of fake crying

I completely believed I would walk through my valley as the writer describes in this passage of scripture.

The days that followed were ~~with~~ filled with nothing but the same. Engulfed with support, love and prayer, fear couldn't find a crack to slip in and discourage me. We shared many precious memories and laughed together. However, one evening resulted in an emotional rage of anger, fear, and weeping.

Cheri was having the most difficult time getting through these days. She still felt responsible. We all struggle with questions trying to figure out why bad things happen to good people, but the blame can't be placed on anyone. Everything bothered her. She became mad, *angry* tense, and very vocal. I understood her fears, but her behavior began to wear down the patience of her brother and sister. Tension continued to mount.

"I don't understand why you can't be here every day," she yelled at her siblings.

"I work too," she said, "but I'm here. Mom needs all of us, and you should know that. I mean, she has cancer for God's sake."

Our son, Aaron, had to drive over an hour to get to the hospital. He worked and took classes at a local college. Dani had just received her graduate degree in biology, and had a new job. Her schedule wasn't as flexible either. I certainly understood both of their circumstances. I know they did everything possible to support their mother, but Cheri felt so angry and bitter toward them. I couldn't understand why.

Soon, tempers flared. They were all exchanging harsh words. Intense feelings rose up and Cheri lost all control of her emotions. Bent over, as if she were in pain or agony, she began to weep. Pouring from her deep brown eyes were huge alligator tears.

She gasped, "But I need you! You don't get it, I need you, both of you."

Because of the dark spiritual state Cheri had been in, along with my unexpected sickness, her faith was exhausted. For the first time ever, she had to admit to Dani and Aaron how she depended on them for strength.

"I'm scared. I don't know what's gonna' happen, and I'm so scared I can't stand it. You have more faith than I do. Dani, you know what the Bible says. You pray a lot and you've always had more faith than me. I don't know what to think. You guys always make me laugh. You just make things better. I can't do this without you. I...I need you."

Some of the things she said were true. Dani and Aaron always had a peculiar sense of humor, hilarious and contagious. Also, Cheri never felt a part of the special bond of sibling companionship the other two seemed to have. When they were young Cheri was always in charge. She wasn't presently in control of anything. Right now, she needed their love, security and closeness; not wanting to face the unknown without them.

Presently, she wasn't

When you share such a close-knit family, you learn to depend on each other. It's only the brash coldness of the world that deceives you into believing you don't need anyone. You think you can do it alone. You begin to believe it and then allow deception to separate you from the ones in your life you truly love. It is humiliating to admit we need someone. We are only little pieces of a greater picture puzzle. When the pieces merge together, you see the whole picture clearer (and) understand. For everything that happens to us there is a reason, a purpose. If we could just humble ourselves to admit we have weaknesses, we can actually get some help. I need you, and you need me. We can face anything and conquer life, together. That's all Cheri was trying to say.

After the shock, drama, and emotional strain, a serene stillness and peace settled in the room. Not another word was said. Cheri sat on the corner of my bed crying quietly. Aaron and Dani both approached her with open arms. No one needed to speak. Just the gesture of acceptance and the assurance of their love and support was all Cheri needed to calm her raging soul, and comfort her frightened heart.

I smile every time I think about that night. We all have issues and hidden fears. When things get resolved, we're better, and the love that binds us together is stronger. These emotional situations were just as challenging as the physical condition I faced daily. Not only did these memorable events stay in my mind, but so many faces stuck with me. Others in the hospital who had the time, no…took the time to make me feel important, or make me feel like I was more than just a case file or subject study.

I remembered in the emergency room a young female doctor with a warm, compassionate personality. She always had a smile and took extra time to talk to me. I knew I could call on her if I had a problem or question, which I did occasionally. She would come every time. She was never afraid to get close enough to hug me. A hug goes a long way. Even if my family wasn't nearby, I never felt alone.

Two other young male residents from urology were always an encouragement. So many times they came to check the edema in my lower body and ask me questions. Or they would wait to see if I had any questions for them. But that last gentle squeeze on my large and swollen toes before leaving the room was a gesture that said they cared. I looked forward to seeing them during the day and will remember their kind faces.

I would love to encourage them to never lose that special touch, or the burden to help and heal. Life becomes stressful and complicated. It's easy to lose sight of the things you love, the commitments you make, and the callings in your life. Any day can throw a curve in the road changing your entire life. The pressures of troubles and trial bring change, but it doesn't have to kill your dreams or aspirations. With God there is always hope for a better future.

8 SURGERY

There we were, all gathered together in my room at five-thirty in the morning. Some of my family spent the night in a home called The House of Care. Family members had access to use this home in the Geisinger complex. All my family showed up. My husband Jim, my daughter, Cheri, with her husband, Mark, my daughter, Danielle, with her husband, Chris, and my son, Aaron, with his wife, Amber.

This was my family, the fruit of the love between a man and a woman, and the wonder God had kept our marriage by His grace for almost thirty years. I looked at my husband. Had I told him enough how much I loved him and appreciated him? All my life he provided for me.

Although he never wanted me to work outside the home, I did hold a part-time job over the last thirteen years. I chose to stay at home when the kids were young. Together we made the sacrifices. We didn't have much, but they were the best years. *While the kids were young, I chose ?*

Through thick and thin, for better or worse, richer, poorer, sickness and health we went through. We were still going through. I looked at my family and my only thought was, "Thank You, Jesus, I am so blessed." A warm feeling of accomplishment came to my mind as I remembered the words to the song, "Butterfly Kisses". I thought of all the times I was so hard on myself for all of the mistakes I made in my life, but surely, I must have done something right.

My father, Ed, sisters, Cindy and Cathy, and my Pastor, Reverend James Bond, and his wife, Jill, also came. I spoke earlier of the special times my dad and I had during this time. My sisters remained faithful also. We suffered with the loss of mom. Now the memories of her complicated surgery were about to resurface.

My Pastor and his wife were such an inspiration, as close as blood relatives to us. They were always there and deeply rooted in our lives. Jill and I share an *emotional* intimacy that is special between sisters. She was in the hospital for surgery a few years ago. Complications surfaced. She needed the Lord desperately to show up on her behalf. Her mother and I were there and began to pray. The Lord heard our plea and delivered her. Her body's system had shut down and the doctors gave her no hope. Once again, God's hand of mercy and healing touch reached into that room. She received divine healing.

There are so many wonderful blessings in the Word of God. When faith grabs hold and melts the heart of God there is no telling what He will do for His people. What a special moment when that thought passed through my mind seeing what God did for her. He was about to do it for me!!

monitored later

sounds like God is holding back

We gathered early before surgery to pray, sing and share hugs and kisses. As much as I loved to sing, lying in bed for so long robbed my strength and I couldn't sing like I wanted to. That didn't matter though, because Jill has a strong soprano voice. Besides, she's the only one I know who can sing that early in the morning, and still sound good. Pastor read scriptures from the Bible. There was no fear in his voice as he read the Bible. I only heard words of confidence and faith, knowing God would complete the work He started in my life. I was not finished here.

It was time to go, but I was not ready. I hadn't been prepared for this. I was in such a spiritual fog I never asked in detail what was going to happen to me. I knew the tumor was too large and complicated to be removed, so they had to remove the kidney with it. I knew this tumor had begun to develop its own vascular system. The vascular surgeon would have his own mess to deal with trying to repair the vena cava, the blood clot, and the damage caused by this massive tumor. We exchanged last kisses and hugs, and never said good-bye, but uttered the words, "See you in a few hours."

Jim and the kids followed as far down the hall as they could. I continued to wave as the attendant wheeled me through the doors of the operating room. I saw their faces as they peered through the small pane of glass while it swiveled back and forth a few times before closing. I loved them so much. I would be back though, and learn to treasure each day as if it were my last. God, please help me to show them love and always be there for them as they were for me. After all, isn't that what love is all about.

There will never be enough words to describe the kind of love that wants to burst through your heart and cover your loved ones with protection from any trouble or evil. We can't do that though. That is why we have Jesus. He is our rock, our shelter, and our fortress. It was His hand I would hold onto now, when theirs couldn't reach beyond the closed doors. It was His hand that would guide each technician, the anesthesiologist, each surgeon and anyone else involved in this procedure. After all, it's His knowledge which gave man the ability to remove this ugly disease called cancer.

I did not feel alone, but for the first time, fear again tried to enter into my heart. God is so amazing. He has a way of coordinating everything in your life. For comfort, He sent another beautiful angel. I don't remember her name, but a special nurse was assigned to help in the pre-op part of my surgery. She explained to me immediately she was a Christian, a believer, and she knew God was with me. Instantly, fear disappeared. Here was another hand to hold, another 'touch' to get me through the next few minutes.

As other nurses and technicians began to explain a few things that were about to happen to me like, prep here, meds there, I had relaxed in the moment of comfort. However, when the suggestion of epidural was mentioned I was ready to get up and run. They tried it. I understood it was in my best interest, but I couldn't tolerate the pain. They gave up. I really felt embarrassed by the fact I could not do this, but they kept on about their business without another word. That is all I can recall before the anesthesia took effect. I found it so comforting the last face I saw before I lost contact with my own consciousness was my angel. God was still in control.

I could only imagine what my family would go through for the next ten hours or so. I still remember the agonizing torture we had to endure during my mother's open-heart surgery. These situations rob you of every bit of strength. They are emotionally draining. Were we going to see the miracle we had longed for? Only time would tell, but I had confidence God was with me, no matter what would follow.

9 RECOVERY

I began to regain consciousness, even though it seemed like a dream. First I heard voices. They weren't clear. The conversation seemed fuzzy and muddled. Someone was arguing whether or not the anesthesia had worn off.

"She's coming out," one whispered.

"No she is not." I heard in a manly voice.

"Yes she is, and it is apparent her breathing is stable," I heard in a clear, louder tone.

I wanted so badly to scream and settle the whole issue for them. I tried to move, but couldn't. Why were my hands tied down? I felt totally helpless, and imprisoned. Wait, the real horror came when I found I couldn't talk, because I had a tube in my mouth…a respirator? Life support? Fear paralyzed me.

Unable to move or speak with no control at all, I thought I'd lose my mind. Did I have the courage to face the recovery ahead? I couldn't describe the awful, choking feeling in my throat. I can't do this. I felt no pain, and didn't want to. This was much more then I bargained for. I never dreamed I had to go through something like this.

I really thought I would die. I guess I wanted to. Oh God, I don't want to stay on life support. What went wrong? Nobody ever mentioned the remote possibility I would end up here, and for how long? Questions kept piercing, searing, roaring through my brain.

Nothing can describe the despair I felt in that moment. The fear of going forward, not knowing what happened, or what I would face created havoc in my spirit. How much of a struggle would I have the next few hours, days, or weeks? How could I face the unknown? It would be so much easier to give up.

Visions of being with my Lord seemed so much more peaceful, joyful and reasonable, than facing the awful future I could dream up on my own. After all, I followed all the instructions in His Word I knew to secure my place in glory with Jesus.

This presented a great opportunity for me to ask the Lord to take me home. I was ready. Most fear death, but I had a promise of eternal life of bliss with Christ with no more pain, or sorrow. The thought was tempting. To meet the Savior face to face seemed like the best option, considering what my immediate future held. To be with Christ is what every believer lives (and dies) for. Our highest goal is to spend eternity with Jesus, worship Him, rest in His arms, and be comforted forever.

Philippians 1:21

For me to live is Christ, and to dies is gain

However, I knew in my heart it wasn't my time to go. The Lord had more plans for my life. He would be able to use my testimony for His glory. I couldn't start to question now. I had to go through this.

Suddenly, a dear brothers' name flashed through my mind, reminding me how much God cares. I remembered Dick, a friend of ours from church. The doctors reported no hope for this man's life. In another hospital across town, his family gathered together. He had a massive heart attack, and suffered so much damage the heart could not be repaired.

Dick already had open-heart surgery a few years before, and this was the end for him. Now on a respirator to keep him alive, his family waited, praying his time would come quickly. This all happened before my admittance to Geisinger hospital. I asked about him often.

One day when Pastor Bond came to visit me, he said he had a letter from a dead man with him. Pastor had just been to visit Dick at the hospital. This man who had no chance at all for recovery came out of a coma. His heart started to work. He motioned for a piece of paper. The only paper Pastor had was a card in his pocket he wanted to give me. Dick began to scribble this question on the envelope, "Where was I when they found me?" So elated with the miracle that took place, Pastor delivered the card to me with Dick's words penned on the envelope. What a demonstration of hope, faith, and a message God does work miracles.

I felt shame to think of leaving my family to be with the Lord too soon. Certainly we look for His appearing, but not to escape. There is too much work to do right here and now. We are stuck with these earthly bodies, but it is for such a brief time. I had to make up my mind I will endure, I will go through. I don't know if it had been the anesthesia, but my thoughts were so scrambled and confused. Nevertheless, I made a promise to Jim I wouldn't leave him.

He had so much passion and emotion in his voice when he begged and pleaded with me, "Please, please don't leave me. Promise me you won't leave me alone. I can't do this without you. I need you. I love you. You're not going anywhere."

I never saw him so fragile, vulnerable and helpless as that day he wept and broke down. Now God is the only one who could help me keep that promise. I would do whatever is necessary. If this was His will for me, I will complete the task no matter how difficult it may be.

Breaking my train of thought, I clearly heard someone say my respirator could be removed. By that time I regained total consciousness. Again, I tried to beg and plead with my eyes, yes, yes, please help me. When I thought it couldn't get any worse, it did.

My family was given permission to visit. They endured twelve hours of agony, pacing, sipping coffee, and tolerating the uncomfortable hospital furniture. Relieved to know I came through the worst; it would do their hearts good to see me. I couldn't respond though, and could only move my eyes. They could only hold my hands through the restraints. That was not comforting. The images I saw that day were heart-breaking.

They came, two by two, all the people I loved and cherished. Their faces reflected shock, discouragement, and fear, but most of all I saw the first glimpse of a lack of faith. Reality hit. I was a gruesome picture, a pale, swollen, bruised, and exhausted vessel. Wife, mother, daughter, sister, and friend, hooked up to monitors, feeding tube, respirator, different IV's, you name it. They were still trying to replenish my blood supply. I lost ten pints of blood during the surgery. My loved ones were not prepared to see me like this. I wished desperately I could have spared them from the pain they suffered watching me.

My husband and father were first to enter the room. Glad to see Jim, I immediately tried to blink my eyes to get his attention, with to avail. He looked tired and worn out. He went through so much. Always the rock of the family, he now had to depend on the kids for support. We had history, and with faith, we could make it through anything.

My eyes drifted over to see dad, stretching his neck around the corner to see me without getting too close. He was hit hardest as tears immediately began to stream down his cheeks. The sight of his baby daughter connected to tubes, IV units, monitors, and other paraphernalia seemed too much for him to handle. He fainted, and stumbled against the cold, hard wall in weakness. I knew he was thinking of mom, his precious wife of almost fifty years. My condition created the same scene he experienced after her surgery, and lost her shortly thereafter. Would he suffer another loss?

Again, if I could only scream! Oh God, who let him in here? Didn't they know? He could have been protected from these emotions. I first thought of his heart, but had to trust God to give daddy the strength to get through this.

Jim took dad out and brought one of my daughters in. I can't remember the order of visitors, but I remember their faces. As each one came in the room I begged with my eyes, and pleaded, take me off this machine. Please help me. Oh God, come to my rescue. I thought, I love you so much my dear family, but I wish you would leave. I cannot stand to look at your faces and watch you agonize over my situation.

One by one they came, my children, their husbands, my sisters, Pastor, and his wife Jill. I tried to blink, twitch, whatever I could to communicate my frustrations, but nothing would change until it was time.

One of my fonder moments while on life-support happened when a friend of mine snuck in to see me. She couldn't have picked a better time. I was feeling pretty low, wallowing in pity. She had a few minutes to pray with me until a nurse found her, and quickly escorted her out.

Being on so much pain medication caused some memories to run together, but I distinctly remember such an amazing peaceful presence throughout the night. With my hand raised high in the air the nurse continually instructed me to put it down. It made the machines go crazy with beeping. She had to keep resetting it. I knew with all my heart, someone was holding my hand. It was so comforting

10 THE APOLOGY

The day after surgery, the most amazing, memorable thing happened. The staff tried hard to keep my visitors to the required limit, but it was difficult to traffic the many people who wanted to visit and pray for me. My father happened to arrive at the right time. Oddly, no one was in my room at the time. It was just the two of us. I was moved into a chair for the moment. The medical staff got surgery patients out of bed and moving around as soon as possible. I certainly understood the concept for muscular profit and circulation. However, I didn't appreciate the extra pain and discomfort. Reluctantly, I did whatever they instructed me to do. I let the nurses maneuver me into whatever positions they thought would be best for me.

My dad sat and watched over me like a guardian angel. Realization set in by this time. He knew he almost lost his baby daughter to this dreadful disease. I still had tubes connected to my body from every angle, but there he sat there quietly and determined to make me comfortable. He was constantly calling the nurses to tend to me. He insisted I was the most important patient in the hospital. He would take the responsibility to ensure they would take extra good care of me. Actually, it was a little overkill. The nurses became a little weary with his demands.

Being a military man all his life, he was very comfortable with giving commands. "Check this," he would say, or "is that supposed to do that...can you make her more comfortable...is that really necessary, why is there a huge tube in her jugular vein...will she be out of ICU soon?" The questions were constant, and annoyed me. I'm sure they saw this type of behavior before. Still, they remained quite patient with him. They listened to his expert medical opinions, and responded to his commands. I appreciated their genuine respect for this seventy-five year old man. With every breath I took, he would jump to offer me an ice chip, rub my dry, parched lips with a cool swab, or fluff my pillow. He could not do enough to make me comfortable. He did a great job nursing me.

Sweet memories of my mother rushed through my mind. All my life it was Mom who nursed me when I was sick. All the chicken soup, liquids, or Vicks Vaporub applications came from her. While Dad was off to work, it was her responsibility to clean up after our sicknesses, tummy aches, and fevers. I am sure he would have gotten the job done, but never had to.

Now it would be up to dad. As painful as this was for him to go through this alone without mom, he would now assume the responsibility to become my nurse and caregiver. Fondly, and ever so lightly, he placed a cool washcloth on my forehead, trying to make me comfortable. He hated seeing me suffer, and like any good father, he would have given anything to help ease my pain. During the beeping of medical equipment, monitors, blood pressure apparatus, and IV drips, a peaceful hush filled the room.

Alone, and in a private moment without interruption, my father began to speak to me. He began to tell me how much he loved me, and what a great daughter I was. Words poured out of his heart. I felt an emotion from him I never experienced. After a few minutes of this emotional expression came a confession I was totally unprepared for.

Out of an absolutely desperate and sincere heart spilled the words of a broken man. He began to weep at my bedside, and apologized for the poor way he treated my husband and me. That had been over thirty years ago.

I met my husband, Jim, at the tender age of fifteen. He was twenty-two. Besides his handsome physical stature, there were other wonderful traits that attracted me to him. He was quiet, polite and the son of a preacher. I immediately introduced him to my parents. *Not really needed ?*

One thing I have yet to mention to my readers is that my husband and I are an interracial couple. That was almost unheard of, and an unacceptable relationship back then.

Anyway, I brought Jim home to meet the parents, hoping they would understand. This young man was nothing but a gentleman and a man of integrity. Much like my own father, Jim worked hard and came from a good family. Surely, before making a decision about the relationship, they would keep an open mind.

My mother's reaction was so sweet, as she asked me for time to think about this. Dad's reaction was totally different with no pondering at all. Actually, as far as he was concerned no compromise was in sight. It was out of the question and there was no further discussion.

Being the typical teenager, I had my mind made up from the beginning. Prejudice never crept into my heart. I could not understand what the problem was. Nevertheless, we proceeded to date, even if I had to hide my feelings. Those days are still vivid in my mind. I never shrank from taking a stand for what's right, and I wouldn't change.

Actually, I shied away from experimenting with drugs, and alcohol wasn't a temptation either. I couldn't stand the taste. Nor did I have the nerve to stay out all night, and purposely hurt or cause worry for my parents. I knew where the lines had been drawn. I had enough sense not to cross them, but in this case, I could not submit to their rules. His ethnicity and culture fascinated me, although with both of us being raised in the same hometown, we weren't different at all.

Okay, I will mention I found Jim strikingly handsome the first time I saw him driving his two-door, nineteen-seventy Ford Mustang past our house. The car had beautiful, bright metallic blue paint, clean white leather interior, and lots of chrome. The shinning, chrome mag wheels caught the sun as he drove down my street. It produced a classic, impressive picture.

weren't all that different ?

Some readers may really disagree, even though you're speaking from your heart

Other than his car, weight lifting was a hobby of his. Jim had a strong, but lean stature. His chest was broad and thick, and the muscular definition in his arms was awesome. He shaped his dark black hair into a perfect seventies afro. He had a clean, stylish look about him.

70's We were raised in the same town, went to the same schools, shopped at the same stores, and had the same likes and dislikes. There weren't many cultural differences to speak of. We had much in common, enjoyed being together, and never lacked good conversation, We both came from good, upstanding families in our local community.

Jim's father was a very reputable minister of the Gospel. He started a church in our little town in 1936. After his death, his mother and family kept the church open. Many knew his mother, brothers, and sisters. They were well known and respected in the community.

My father, Ed, had been a part of the Armed Forces for most of his life. He was a dedicated, disciplined man of integrity. Everyone knew him. After all, his mother and brother owned and operated Hoch's Restaurant, one of the first diners in Milton. Their home cooking was known far and wide.

Everyone today throws around the word 'dysfunctional' with ease, but you couldn't convince me there was anything dysfunctional about my family. In my mind as a child growing up, we were perfect and happy. It broke my heart to hurt my parents with disobedience, but their worst hardship and grief came from our community, (so-called) friends, and neighbors. Even an occasional slur would come from a family member.

I will give my parents all of the credit they deserve. They taught me not to see differences in people. They taught me how to truly love and respect others. Whether people are racially, socially, or economically different, every life is valuable. I grew up with the idea we are all the same, and not one person is better than the other. Diversity was welcome in my heart and mind. I was bent on making friends with anyone. I believed in the principle we are all created equal, but my family just couldn't accept my new relationship. For whatever reasons, they could not find the courage to practice what they taught me.

I often look back and think my life would make a great movie. I hoped things would get better, and people would change. God created mankind. We are all equal in His sight. The Lord gave Jim and I so much strength and unity as a couple, it didn't matter what others think. A family is an institution created by God. The love of a husband and wife is an example of Christ's love for the church.

The brothers and sisters I also call my family have proven themselves by their actions of love and devotion during my sickness. I have to say yes, some things do change. It's a 'God' thing, and His Spirit completes this ultimate transformation of the mind, which enables us to love each other unconditionally.

Regardless, my father was not pleased. For the next three years Jim and I struggled to hold onto our relationship. After I turned eighteen we were married at the church I grew up in. Even the reverend that performed the ceremony experienced persecution from our small town. Within the year he was transferred.

On that special day, our wedding day, it rained all morning. It was a warm, steady, and gentle rain though, which felt fresh, even cleansing. With a small handful of friends as our witnesses, we began our journey through life together. At that point, daddy had disowned me. There was no communication between the two of us for the following three years.

We prayed for a change. We believed God once again for a miracle, and a change of heart. The next few years went by quickly. Our first girl, Cheri, was born. Dad knew it, but remained stubborn and closed to a relationship with his own daughter and grandchild. After two years, our second little girl, Danielle, came into our lives.

Then, on Cheri's third birthday, something amazing happened. Other than pictures, my father never saw either one of his granddaughters. My mother was allowed to visit us and she did, faithfully. She never missed a birthday, Christmas, Easter, or any other holiday. She worked at a local dress shop, and made sure Cheri and Dani had new shoes to wear whenever they needed them. The children and I were always welcome at my parents home, but only if dad was not there.

Being the disciplined man he was, Dad never veered from his schedule. He left for work at seven-thirty every morning, after his morning cup of coffee. He would then stop at the Post Office to pick up the office mail, and come home promptly at twelve forty-five for lunch.

Mom had invited the girls and me down to her house in the morning to give Cheri a birthday gift. Cheri was so delighted to receive a new, shiny, red tricycle from her grandmother. We were very aware of the time, and realized dad would be home soon, so I began to get the girls' coats on. Just as we were about to leave, dad came home early for lunch. My heart skipped a beat, for I knew something went wrong. He never come home early for lunch. It wasn't part of his routine, and besides, he knew we were there.

The door opened, he took off his hat and coat, set them aside, and walked upstairs. The first words to come out of his mouth were, "Happy birthday Cheri," as he turned the corner, waved at her, and continued into the kitchen to get his lunch. Mom and I were dumbfounded and just stared at each other. Quickly, and without a word, somehow we both knew we should go along with this. No questions were in order, and no doubt entered our thoughts. This is what we had been waiting and praying for.

God in His awesome and mysterious ways performed a miracle right in front of our eyes. He proved to me once again, He could do absolutely anything. Restoration and reconciliation is what He is all about. That's why He sent His Son to die for us. Why should I have been surprised? This is what we were praying for.

Not even a minute passed before I removed the coats from the kids. Cheri made a little loop around the living room.

Gleaming, she exclaimed, "You like my bike?"

She was so proud of her new red tricycle. She wanted to show it to 'Pop-Pop'. Conversation came so easy, natural, and sincere it seemed like the last few years I missed with my father never happened. The past hurt, rejection, pain, the praying and waiting, were all over in a split second. After that moment, life went on as if nothing ever happened. We sat, ate lunch together, and said good-bye. Then dad left to resume his usual, daily routine.

Since that day, our family grew even closer. We became a family in every sense of the word, and could live and love freely. Like every other close-knit family, we shared every aspect of life. The best thing about my miracle was no bitterness or unforgiveness remained. Not once did Jim or I expect an apology or explanation from dad, concerning his actions and rejection from the previous years. Jim certainly could have been the kind of person to be stubborn, and require some kind of acknowledgement he had been wronged in the situation, but he wasn't. The picnics, birthday parties, and family activities resumed as if communication was never broken.

It didn't matter, because I had my father's love. I always knew he still loved me, but needed time to accept the situation. God needed time to speak to his spirit and heal his heart. The Lord wanted to let him know his own family was more important than his pride. I am a witness of God's power of persuasion.

After that moment in time, my father became a real help to us. The many years we were married, he never questioned when we needed support of any kind. He was there loving, giving, and sharing whatever he could, whether it was his finances or to help around the house with a hammer or power tool.

Both dad and mom loved to hear our singing group. Gospel and Christian music was new to them. They both embraced it with joy. Nothing made them prouder than to attend one of our concerts at a local church, enjoy our music, and hear the sweet voices of their grandchildren singing, "Yes Jesus Loves Me". Their tears of gladness replaced all the tears of sadness I shed during dad's absence in my life..

I'm grateful for the path my life took. It lead me to the richest and most fulfilling relationship with Christ I could ever dream of. It's Christ that brought my family back together again. His love and total purpose, allowed Jim and I to meet.

On that special day in Intensive Care, I lay helpless, hooked up to machines, and listened as my father poured out this sincere confession of the heart. He was so ashamed to think he didn't give Jim a chance from the start. He recognized he hadn't treated him right. Almost thirty years had passed, and he never mentioned a word of his true feelings.

Now he was asking for forgiveness. Somewhere, somehow, dad needed closure. My father softened, watching the many great blessings of the Lord in my life. I believe he responded with incredible sensitivity. He uttered praises about my husband, and recognized Jim as a faithful, loving, and supportive husband. As his voice broke, and the tears streamed down his face, he tried to tell me Jim was a good man and never deserved that kind of hateful treatment and rejection.

"Please forgive me," dad begged. "I just can't believe it." He continued, "Nobody deserved that. I'm so sorry for what I did to the both of you. You know I love you with all my heart. I don't know what I was thinking. I love all my girls. I'm so sorry."

Listening to him, watching him sit there and sob and say over and over again how sorry he was seemed more than I could handle. With tubes down my nose and throat, I couldn't speak to him, or console him. The only communication I had were the tears dropping out of the corner of my eyes, forming small pools inside my ears. I was in shock. Was this one of the reasons this happened to me? I never imagined how this tragedy could affect the hearts of the people I love so dearly. It wasn't I considered dad to be too hard or insensitive to apologize, but I never expected it, asked for it, or needed it.

In my heart, the Lord fixed the situation, and reconciled my relationship with my father. That was enough for me. All I wanted was for him to be part of my life. God answered those prayers. For whatever reason, dad needed to make things right. I allowed him the opportunity. It was truly an emotional, soul-bearing confession. I've never experienced such a heart-felt apology.

If I saw his heart at that moment, I would have seen a picture of a beautifully, clean swept room, a place as fresh as the summer breeze, and a place where God's mercy and grace flowed freely from the throne of God. I would never dare to compare my emotions with God's, but I have a real good idea of how our Godly Father feels when we come to Him in absolute humbleness. A broken and contrite spirit God will never turn away.

Psalm 34:18

The Lord is nigh unto them that are of a broken heart; and saveth such as he of a contrite spirit

Psalm 51:17

…a broken and a contrite heart, O God, thou wilt not despise.

Things in our past may mean nothing to anyone else, but they're wrapped up tightly inside us. Our feelings are just waiting to be revealed and poured out from within to a loving Father and Savior. He is the only one who has the absolute power to forgive and forget. There are no choices but for Him to forgive, because it's His promise. His Word was established, and doesn't change. What an incredible, cleansing experience. It's available for all of us.

I wouldn't trade that genuinely innocent, tender moment for anything in the world. This chapter in my life will be remembered as one of the most moving, sincere, and inspirational events that ever took place.

It all happened while laid up in the hospital. After a drastic surgery, God moves things in the spiritual world we can't comprehend. We don't always see what the Lord is doing on our behalf. Be certain, however, He is doing something. When God does it, it's done right. He doesn't need our help. Nobody will ever be able to tell me God cannot change someone's heart. No circumstance is so hard God can't fix it. There is no need too great, our great provider cannot supply. There is no pain He can't comfort. There is no disease He cannot heal. There is no wrong He can't make right. I am preaching to myself right now. There are days I have to encourage myself.

There is amazing hope in knowing our loving Father, Provider, Savior, and FRIEND. I want to share this testimony, because there are so many other hurting people. I know we often hurt each other, but usually not intentionally. I will always remember and cherish this moment and tender confession. Restoration and true reconciliation are gifts given us by God. I want to encourage others and let them know He does the same for everyone. He cares about every little detail of our lives. If we allow Him, He will prove it. Just like He did concerning the relationship between my father and I.

11 MORE RECOVERY

Within forty-eight hours, I was taken off the ventilator. Thankfully, the spark of faith began to show in the eyes of my family again. I was out of the intensive care unit and in step down. I was out of immediate danger. The feeding tube was the next obstacle to overcome. Morphine worked very well. I had very little pain. I was cut from one side of my abdomen up to the middle of my chest and back down the other side of my stomach. It looked like a large, v-shaped railroad across the front of my body. I counted forty-nine staples. Still swollen, I couldn't move left or right. I didn't dare to lift my head to see my toes.

Every day brought a new adventure. Today's mortifying feat was to sit in a chair. The nurses would not let me rest until this was accomplished. They all grabbed the corners of the blanket underneath my body and flung me into a recliner. I sat for the rest of the day and dreaded the move back to bed. I learned quickly how to use the little button to administer more morphine and began clicking as soon as I saw them coming. This time it took an extra person to lift me back into the hospital bed.

The next day's adventure was to walk. I didn't know how that would happen. I didn't have the ability to move any part of my body, let alone try to walk. I understood the necessity of getting muscles to move, but with the swelling I couldn't even get both legs between a walker, nor bend them. After pushing me out of bed onto my feet I was horrified by what took place next.

They put a large walker as big as a treadmill in front of me and leaned me up against it. Then they proceeded to push it around the room. I still laugh to myself thinking of how funny it must have looked. Everyone began to applaud and remark how well I was walking, which was an outright lie. My legs somehow slid across the floor, but I wasn't walking on my own. They were happy enough to let me sit back down in my chair, pushing my little button with every movement. I know they monitored the morphine, but I clicked that thing so often it should have broken!

The next day or so I learned morphine might hinder the healing process. I stopped using it. I needed to get on with my life, and out of there. I would sacrifice pain to do it. The feeding tube hadn't been a problem, just an inconvenience. It must have worked, for I hadn't eaten in days, and wasn't hungry.

However, I needed a drink. My lips had split from being chapped and dry. All I wanted was a tiny piece of ice, not a cotton swab running across the rough splinters of my mouth leaving small particles of cotton. I begged.

Finally, one of the young Doctors who came routinely to check on me found someone in authority to authorize ice chips. What a sweetheart!

I remember begging for the feeding tube to be removed. Yes, I know its purpose. They were listening for more activity in my stomach, but I still pleaded. My young friend once again came to my rescue. He talked to the head physician, and against his better judgment he agreed to remove it.

As the doctor entered the room, my resident friend stood at the end of the bed and winked at me.

The head doctor stated, "We'll give this a try, but I want you to know, if you're stomach isn't ready, we'll have to put it back in."

He showed his displeasure by grabbing the tube and practically ripping it from my nose. Tears filled my eyes, but I choked back any comments that crossed my mind. I was just glad to get rid of it.

My resident friend left the room with a smile on his face. I thanked God for sending me another angel to help me through the process.

The first week in the hospital, I had a private room. I had so much company, the nurses called it the party room. They were very patient with the crowds, noise and activity, even after visiting hours.

After the surgery, I was moved to a new section of the hospital. I shared a larger, much nicer room with two other women, Until I was moved to a special facility for rehab, this would be my home for a week.

One of the women in the room was in an accident eleven years ago. They were still doing surgery on her face and nose. I didn't know the accident left her blind until I saw her grope along the wall or bed to find the bathroom. She was in constant pain, but never complained. Even though she'd never see her two children grow up, her spirits were always good.

Again, I concentrated my prayers for her and was lifted out of my own pity party. I quickly regained the heart to praise God for His many blessings toward me. After all, my prognosis was good. I would recover from this. At least I could see my precious grandchildren and had an overwhelming sense of hope I would play with them again.

I couldn't understand why the swelling was so bad. They reassured me it would decrease, but I had my doubts. I couldn't move my legs more than an inch per step. The catheter had to remain until the swelling began to subside.

Cheri, my new guardian angel, had all of my calls held. She insisted there would be no more visitors for a while. At first I was upset, but I couldn't even reach the telephone. A hospital is not the best place to have peace and quiet, but I did appreciate not having continual visitors. I needed the time to rest and heal. I missed my friends coming to visit, but they should be spared the embarrassment of seeing me in the fine linen the hospital gave me to wear.

Slowly, tubes were disconnected. Even the doctors seemed amazed

confusing

things were going so well, considering the extent of the surgery I went through. At this point I had no appetite. Yet, fear of another feeding tube kept me eating. They didn't want me to go home yet. They knew I couldn't walk and wouldn't be able to take care of even simple daily tasks. They recommended a facility nearby for rehabilitation, but had to wait until the catheter was removed.

Only twenty-four hours passed since they gave the okay to remove it. Once again, all my things were transferred and shoved into bags to go home. During my three-week stay at the hospital I accumulated so many flowers, gifts, stuffed animals, cards, books and CD's. I had no idea what my home would look like when I got back, or if I would be able to find anything when I got there. My family took good care of everything. They never complained about the extra workload.

12 REHABILITATION

I apprehensively looked forward to the next phase of recovery. I couldn't walk yet, so I faced the challenge of learning how to maneuver a wheelchair. I appreciated my family who did a great job of transferring all my cards, gifts, and paraphernalia. Because my lower body was still very swollen, none of my regular clothes fit. The girls bought some extra large pajamas for me to wear to my new home.

It had rained the day before, but the clouds rolled away, leaving the day cool and breezy. A couple blankets snuggly tucked around me kept me warm and comfy for the ride. Upon arrival, we were greeted by a wonderful staff of nurses. There were plenty of smiles and encouragement to go around. These people were as accommodating as the staff at the hospital, but I had been warned. They'd make me work extremely hard.

I've often heard you never know what you're missing until it's gone. It became painfully true for me. It's amazing to think of all of the things I took for granted every day. To have someone teach you how to get out of bed in the morning is very humbling. I wondered why God would ever put up with the many times I grumbled and complained.

At rehab, I would be taught how to take care of myself with my temporary disabilities. I had to be lifted out of bed into a chair and have someone give me a bath or wash my hair. Even going to the bathroom became an impossible task for me. It was so embarrassing to ask for help with something so private. I felt I didn't belong there, but there wasn't anywhere else to go besides a nursing home.

There weren't many younger or middle-aged patients there to receive therapy. I felt out of place. Most patients were older with heart problems and hip replacements. Every day they pressed through different types of therapy, needing help to walk, dress and perform other daily chores. One young man in his early twenties was left paralyzed from a terrible car accident. They worked diligently with him every day. Even if it took three or four people to carry him, they never let up. Patiently and gently they placed one foot in front of another. They helped him move his legs and arms while shifting him back and forth encouraging him to walk. Over and over, every day they would repeat this procedure. They had total confidence and faith they would be able to help him.

Another inspirational young man lost his leg due to a work injury. He had a great attitude despite the obstacles he faced. I saw him work so hard in learning how to adjust with the loss of his limb. He struggled every day to strengthen the rest of his body which he had to depend on to get him

61

around. He only wanted to go home to his wife and children and resume his life to the best of his ability. I ask God to help me remember these individuals and keep them in my prayers. Looking around, I saw people like myself struggling to get their lives back.

Hope kept me going during my long, difficult road to recovery. My family and friends would not let me forget His promises. Kim, a member of our church ministry team, always brought words of encouragement. She helped me regain my vision of life after crisis.

One memorable, but emotional experience happened after my first full day at the clinic. My daughter and grandchildren were taking me for a stroll in my wheelchair when I noticed Kim walking toward me from the end of the hall. I began to weep. Uncontrollable sobbing hadn't been a part of my routine, but something in my spirit broke. Sitting in the hallway, I tried so hard to remain strong in the presence of my little granddaughters. I didn't want to scare them, or let them see me in such a weak state of mind. Quickly discerning my emotional state, Cheri quietly ushered the kids back to my room and to their daddy until I could get myself together.

Kim has an amazing ability to encourage and inspire others through God's Word. She's always had a sensitivity and intuition toward my mood swings and emotional needs. I never perceived Kim as a mother image, but that's the emotion that gripped me the closer she came. Feelings from the past rushed over me. I just sobbed.

I felt like a little girl again. Anytime I made a mistake, or was hurt, I didn't want anyone to see me cry. As soon as I saw mom, my walls crumbled. Her presence seemed to melt my spirit, not as a sign of weakness, but it showed her amazing strength and nurturing. I knew as soon as I was wrapped in the loving warmth of mom's arms, everything would be okay and the pain would subside. I never needed to hide behind pride, or use a false face with mom. That tactic is a defense mechanism, so no one can see the pain. I could always be myself with Mom, a comfortable place I longed to return to.

What a beautiful peace I remembered so well, in my mother's loving arms. I never had to pretend. I knew I was always loved and accepted, no matter what the circumstances were. A caring mother picked you up, cleaned the wound, bandaged and kissed the boo-boo. I know I had something special as a child and thank God for the mother I had.

Kim had no idea what was going through my mind. She had a keen sensitivity though, and used her gift to encourage my heart and calm my spirit.

"Oh God, how did I get here? How am I going to do this?" I sobbed.

"Come on, things will work out," she responded. "This is just a small piece of the puzzle. It will all fall into place, believe me. You're doing great. There's nothing to be afraid of. Just take a deep breath."

Sometimes long speeches aren't necessary. One smile or touch can be encouraging and bring things back into focus. Kim was very good at prioritizing. She helped put things in their proper place. She always had insight into the mixed up stuff that went on in my life. Everything happens for a reason. God sees it and allows things to happen for our faith and growth. Many times we bring things onto ourselves by not listening, or by breaking the rules. Other times we find ourselves facing circumstances in our lives that actually help us mature in Christ.

After many tears, a deep sigh and a big hug, I soon regained my composure. This situation was temporary. Things would work out. As she put her arms around me, I felt peace. Much like my mother's love, the Lord wanted to hold me, calm my fears, dry my tears, and comfort me. I had to let my family and friends stand in the gap for me when my faith was weak. I was there for others, and stood strong in faith for their needs. Now it was time for me to receive and let them hold me up. Every day I spent at rehab is stored in my memory. I thank God for the special people He sent to lift my spirits and build my faith.

Another couple from church came to visit bringing joy, cheer, and lots of balloons. They arrived dressed up as clowns. As part of their children's ministry, they traveled to different churches and community events sharing this gift. They created hats, flowers, and animals out of the bright, colorful balloons. They lit up the day with their art and unique ministry. My grandchildren happened to be there. To see their eyes light up reminded me of Christmas Day. This event was all happening around their "Mimi," who could barely bend over to give them a hug, but the moment was awesome.

Once again the room filled with conversation, laughter and boisterous noise as we shared and were blessed by the people of God. We thought for sure a grievance would be made because of the noise and sounds of celebration coming from my room, but we never heard a complaint from anyone. The nurses, who came in on a regular basis to check my stats, were even swept up in the joy of the moment. They would thank me for letting them be a part of our special experience. I sensed a hunger in their spirits. Everyone wants to be included or part of something greater than them.

They enjoyed my visitors and knew we were a different bunch, a peculiar people. They particularly enjoyed the outdoor worship service my friends and family brought to me.

The facility received donations to erect an outdoor gazebo. A windy, red brick path led down into beautiful gardens of flowers and greens to where the gazebo sat. The last several days were very dreary, rainy, and cold. The fresh air softly blowing through the trees on this warm, sunny day became a welcome change from the inside of my room.

It was so touching to see everyone. My church family, along with Jim, dad, sister, her husband, and my children, were all a part of our small, outdoor service. Our music and worship team brought a CD. We sang along with the music, clapping and lifting our hands. We worshipped the Lord while the warmth of the sun covered us like a cozy electric blanket. We had church outside under the gray-white clouds that powdered the sky. It reminded me of the children of Israel as they traveled through the wilderness. The presence of God was always there to cover and protect them with a cloud by day and a pillar of fire by night.

Exodus 13:21

And the Lord went before them by day in a pillar of a cloud,
to lead them the way; and by night in a pillar of fire,
to give them light; to go by day and night.

Suddenly, I felt very secure, very safe, under the ceiling of His throne. The warmth of the sun and the formation of the clouds gave me a picture of His hands in my life. The prayers of my friends were always so comforting. Even their children were a blessing to me. Quaylin, a precious two-year old, came over to me, placed my hand in his and gently squeezed it. He stood with me for the longest time. His eyes pierced mine as if to say, "See, you're okay." I could imagine God smiling from the heavens. God bless this dear child.

I longed to stand in His presence as innocent as him without doubt, trusting God for everything in my life. I never questioned in my childhood where food, clothing, or shelter would come from. I just knew those provisions would be made. I wanted to be like one of those little ones that day, trusting Him completely with that same child-like faith. Outside the cool, brick exterior of the clinic walls we felt love. You could not only feel it, but the expressions on the faces of God's people reflected true peace.

People peered out of the building in curiosity. To hear the singing clearer, some cracked the windows of their rooms. Others walked by and smiled. We began to sing and rejoice even louder, inviting the world into this wonderful celebration. The children played and sang along too. We spent the best part of an hour praising God together. He added to our faith and bound our hearts together in love. I enjoyed this true expression of fellowship and unity, but the reality of my condition soon hit me. It was time to get back to bed. My legs were swollen and aching, my body hurt, but I had been spiritually refreshed and was ready to face the future.

Back inside my room I faced reality again. I had a vigorous schedule to keep up with and therapy was no picnic. No longer did anyone offer to assist me with my bath. I couldn't bend to reach my feet, so they gave me a device that had a long handle with a sponge attached to the end. Warm water and towels were provided. I was on my own.

When the staples were removed, I was able to take a shower. I cried because it had been so long. It felt soothing and relaxing just to sit, and let the warm, massaging water roll down my back, and over my poor, puffy, cut up body. What relief! To brush my teeth, I could at least swing the wheelchair over to the sink and also comb my hair in the mirror. Then I'd wheel myself down the hallway to the fitness room where I would begin my daily regimen of exercise.

The worst part of therapy was trying to walk. I started out with twenty-five steps and had to work up to fifty. At that point, fifty steps seemed impossible for me. I still couldn't get both legs between the walker because of the swelling, and couldn't bend my knees. I felt like my skin would tear and explode at any minute. Just standing for a few minutes built more pressure and discomfort. I questioned the therapists often, saying, "When will the swelling go down" and, "do you realize I still have blood clots?"

I couldn't wait to get back to my wheelchair between short walks to prop my legs up again. The breaks to rest between exercises were brief. The total duration of my treatment consisted of an hour of therapy. Then, tired and worn out, I'd return to my room and struggle to get into bed. I had to position my legs upright for the rest of the day.

One day our son, Aaron, came to rehab to observe my therapy. During my session, the therapist had me work on the fifty steps I needed to accomplish. I walked from where my wheelchair sat to another place in the room and back again. Aaron felt sorry for me. He stared at me with this sad look as if he could cry at any moment. His response was so endearing. A water cooler sat in the corner with small paper cups that held about two sips of water. After every trip I made around the room, there stood Aaron, waiting and bearing a fresh cup of water each time I crossed the finish line.

Our roles had been reversed. He was now the proud and encouraging parent, waiting to render words of encouragement and applause to my accomplishments. This small cup of water was a reward for all my hard work. He saw the effort it took to press through the pain in walking those few steps. This was the only way he could find to bring his mom comfort.

Those were the moments that helped me face the struggles I had day after day. Each therapy session brought a new exercise, or form of torture, with parallel bars, weights, and sit-ups. It was a feat to close my eyes, lift one leg in a standing position, and try to stay balanced in the meantime. I never thought keeping my balance would be such a huge accomplishment. It seemed as if I would never be able to return to normal.

However, I did begin to see small improvement in my muscles every day. My body began to respond to this regiment. With great determination, I managed to walk up a set of three steps.

Impressed with my progress, my therapist was ready to take this information to the weekly meetings, when they review their patient's progress. They would then decide whether or not I could be discharged. I had more mobility and could get out of bed. I could now hobble to the shower and lower myself to a sitting position.

The doctors were mainly concerned about the stairway going up to the second floor of our home. We didn't have railing to help me climb the stairs. We assured them I would have ample help.

My family would be there to see I'd be safe in my own home. My husband planned to take a week off work, and our children were as faithful as clockwork. I could walk without bringing the walker into my small bedroom. I worked hard to achieve fifty steps and I could get to the bathroom without it.

Not happy with the thought of discharging me, Cheri began to complain. She thought it might be too early for me to go home. She was really concerned about getting the house ready. She wanted to have everything special, cleaned, ready, and in perfect order before my arrival. With working and visiting, she had no time to prepare my house.

Nobody did. Everyone was so busy traveling the roads to visit me there was hardly enough time to take care of their own homes, let alone mine. I didn't expect to come home to a perfectly clean house. I just wanted to go home. A little dust never hurt anyone. It would get cleaned all in good time. I'm sure her reservations were predicated upon the fear that I may not have adequate help. She wanted to make sure I would be comfortable and happy

Nevertheless, I was ready to go home. To help ease the doctor's minds, I successfully performed every personal task required of me. I still couldn't dress without help, but hadn't planned on going out of the house or making any trips in the near future. Certainly, I felt apprehension about going home, but not fearful. I just wanted to be surrounded by my things, get in my bed, and use my own bathroom.

The staff had all been so kind, but there's no place like home and no company better than family. Besides, there were only forty beds in the rehab clinic and someone else had a far greater need for their service than I did.

The physicians and therapists were pleased, ordered my discharge, and the process began. My doctor came in and removed all my staples as soon as she heard I would be going home. I dreaded the experience, but after what I went through, a little extra pain was nothing. I had no feeling in the area of my incision, or my entire stomach. So to my surprise, I only felt a pinch or two from the removal of the staples.

She explained the process; the nerve endings in that area would reconnect approximately one-sixteenth inch per month. The incision looked like a kangaroo's pouch. They cut the front of my body open to get inside, shoved other organs around, and removed my right kidney. The large, cancerous monster of a tumor had begun to consume it, then additional surgery was required to repair the major vein the tentacles of this octopus-like form had invaded. Also, a large portion of blood clot had built up in both legs from being immobile the week prior to surgery. The medical team then closed and zipped me up. It was definitely not a pretty sight to see. The scar will never let me forget. It's so incredible to think God gave mankind the ability to perform such an awesome task. Just to think of how my muscle, tissue, and nerves were cut and severed, yet will heal in time amazed me.

What is more astounding, we were created with such an intricate system the human body is equipped to mend and heal itself. The resources available to us today are phenomenal. I can't even fathom what technology the future holds. God designed a marvelous brain within us, and there is so much more to be explored and revealed.

Psalms 139: 14

I will praise thee for I am fearfully and wonderfully made:
marvelous are they works; and that my soul knoweth right well.

Doctors cannot control who lives or dies. Only our Master, our Creator, has that right. I thank God for allowing me to live, because I deem it a wonderful privilege and honor. I will share my testimony whenever I have the opportunity and remind people tomorrow is not promised. Doctors can fix just about anything today, but they can't fix the heart, or the soul of a man. Only God, Himself, can repair the state of man's soul.

There is hope though, through Jesus Christ His only son. We can take steps to insure reconciliation. The Bible talks about a spiritual circumcision of the heart, a process where the old nature of man is removed.

13 HOME SWEET HOME

The trip home was delicate. All the cards, gifts, flowers, and CD's in my room were packed up again, this time for home. They escorted me in the wheel chair to our van. Trying to maneuver swollen, stiff legs into the van caused more pain and discomfort, but it didn't matter. The edema made me feel like I was tightly stuffed into an undersized, one-piece snow-skiing outfit. I had no flexibility at all to sit or bend.

Cheri used pillows to prop me up and try to make me comfortable. It took a while to lift, slide, and shimmy, but finally I reached a somewhat comfortable position in the front seat. Already stressed, as we began to move it became worse. I felt every organ in my body shake and tremble with every little bump and turn in the road.

We had to make one stop before heading home to pick up medication. I sat in the van while Jim went in the store. I adjusted the tuner of the radio to a Christian station which played old-style gospel music. While relaxing and enjoying the program, they began to play a familiar recording of "The Lighthouse". While listening to the different arrangement of the song, I couldn't stop the tears landing on the front of my sweater. I hadn't even tried to sing during the last several weeks. Because of the surgery, the respirator, and all I went through, my throat had become weak and sore.

At first I began to whisper, trying not to put a strain on my voice. The tears were streaming down my face by now. My voice began to grow louder and louder. Soon I was having my own concert; just me and Jesus.

I was so relieved to know I had not lost something beautiful God gave me. It didn't matter if anyone heard me, or if I looked odd sitting in the car and enjoying this moment by myself. The vehicle had become full of the Spirit of God and I felt a sweet release. I had an encounter with God while sitting in the Wal-Mart parking lot.

The first thing Jim saw when he got into the car were my tears. I reassured him they were tears of joy and shared my experience with him. Thrilled my voice was coming back, we rejoiced together on the way home. With the car filled with a sweet spirit, we enjoyed the remainder of our trip home. Any fear or apprehensions I had diminished and I looked forward to facing the obstacles ahead of me.

As soon as we pulled up to the house, we noticed one of our good friends waiting in the driveway. The ladies at church had meals lined up to be delivered to us for the next two weeks. Dinner was hot and ready. Even during my stay at the hospital people brought food to the house so Jim had something to eat. I had everything I needed to get through the next phase of healing.

The steps up to the house were easy to climb. My favorite couch awaited me right inside the door. I rested there for quite a while before going upstairs. I actually crawled up the stairway like a toddler, but successfully made it to the top with no problem. Now the only job I had to do was rest, which I did with ease. We lived one mile from where Jim worked. Every day he'd come home to fix me two eggs, toast, and a glass of Tang. I enjoyed my brunch brought to my bedside. He always looked so eager and pleased to care for me.

Because we only had the one bathroom upstairs, I ventured downstairs once a day. We had a large window in the front of our home. In the afternoon, I would sit by the window and enjoy the sunlight. The neighbors would come by and talk with me. I took sick so quickly most of them never knew what had happened to me. They were shocked.

During that time at home, the lawn got mowed, the house was cleaned, the dishes washed, and the laundry did not back up. We certainly didn't lack for food either.

I was feeling better every day, but swelling in the lower part of my body was still an issue. It took a lot of strength to get up from the bed. I missed the adjustable hospital bed. The strain of maneuvering without using any stomach muscles damaged my left shoulder. I never felt it because of the pain medication I had been taking. I began to notice it when I started to decrease my dosage, but that would heal with time also.

After a week Jim returned to work. Financially we needed him to get back to his job. My employer had offered no unemployment or workers compensation benefits to help replace my lost income. We never discussed the budget, but I knew it was a primary concern for him. God had never failed us so we chose to pray and trust Him.

The grace of God continued to shower in our lives. Monetary gifts from both our families, along with others from the church began pouring in. Someone called our electric company and deposited enough money to cover the next three months of service. We received a sizable donation, which helped us with the mortgage payments for a while. Jim's friends and co-workers collected an offering to help out also.

One title for God in the Bible is Jehovah Jireh, which means He is our provider. Once again God proved Himself to be our provider.

Genesis 22:14

And Abraham called the name of that place Jehova Jjireh: as it is said to this day. In the mount of the LORD it shall be seen. (KJV)

So Abraham called that place The LORD Will Provide. And to this day it is said, "On the mountain of the LORD it will be provided. (NIV)

Experiencing the Lord fill my life with everything I needed left me with an incredible desire to return to the worship and fellowship I missed desperately.

However, the preparation just to get dressed and out of the house would be an ordeal. For the first time I tried on something other than my oversized pajamas. Everything fit loosely because of the weight I had lost. Dressing didn't cause any difficulties, but every step down the stairs and out of the house brought the realization that this trip would yield consequences I may not enjoy. Nevertheless, I grabbed extra medication in case the pain became overwhelming.

The reunion with my church family was emotional but rewarding. Emotional because I couldn't sing as loudly and boisterous as I normally would. My spirit wanted to burst out with praise for all God had done for me, but I physically couldn't. All my stomach muscles had been severed. It would take months before I'd be myself again.

Traditional wooden pews lined our church from front to back. A cushioned chair had been brought in just for my comfort. The service was moving and stirring. My friends were grateful to see me back for the first time. My victory seemed to be the inspiration for the selection of songs for the service, even the Pastor's message.

One by one they came to me with hugs, kisses, and tears. Everyone expressed his or her gratitude to the Lord for saving my life. They knew the healing process was not over and helped lift me up by speaking more words of life into my spirit. The familiar feeling of love I experienced that morning blessed me and helped keep me through the week, lingering like the fragrance of fresh flowers.

Flashbacks of a wonderful, refreshing childhood memory popped into my mind. Mrs. Burns, a delicate and fragile elderly woman loved her flowers. The front yard of her house consisted of lush gardens containing every bloom imaginable. A small, slate walkway resembling a winding, country brook went down through the middle of her yard. It provided the narrow divider which parted the vibrant, beautiful medley of colors. I could smell the perfume of this earthly splendor through my bedroom window, as the fragrance rose with the soft, summer breeze. I took in a deep breath; back home again with my family.

The next few weeks went by quickly. More strength came with each day. I looked forward to leading worship again. After two weeks I sat on the platform on a small stool. I started living, breathing, and doing what came so natural to me again. I was back, and ready to stand on the front line.

In the Old Testament of the Bible, the musicians and singers led the people of God into battle with their ministry of hymns, spiritual songs, dance, and shouting.

2nd Chronicles 20: 21

And when he had consulted with the people, he appointed singers unto the Lord, And that should praise the beauty of holiness, as they went out before the army, And to say, Praise the Lord; for his mercy endureth for ever.

Before I knew it, summer had passed. Thank God, the edema finally began to subside, but the doctors told me my circulation would never be the same. I wasn't to sit or stand for any length of time. I had to wear knee-high compression hose daily so the swelling wouldn't be too bad. My legs still got puffy by the end of the day, but I was alive and not complaining.

I began to journal about what I went through. I wrote about my physical sickness, along with my mental, emotional, and spiritual condition. I should have done this all along, but considering the state I was in, I couldn't. The words that were bottled up inside me for the past four months started pouring out, day and night. I couldn't sleep because thoughts, words, faces, and the strong feelings from what I went through kept me stirring and tossing in bed. Page after page, paragraphs, and whole chapters accumulated so fast. I had no idea I had so much to say.

As I sat at my home computer, my fingers couldn't keep up with the river of words flowing from my heart. The doctor's instructions slipped from my mind. Unfortunately, the more I wrote, the more the skin on my feet and legs felt like it was burning, and tight. Looking down I saw both legs, thick with swelling again, even with the compression hose on.

So we bought our first laptop. Doing my work with my feet propped up helped alleviate some of the problem. I was determined to tell my story and share the most personal sentiments of my heart, including the most intimate accounts with my family and what God did in my life. I wanted to give back to Him, with hope someone else would receive encouragement and help from my testimony.

14 MOVING FORWARD

My message is clear. God's people reflect His character and personality in this world. My music, service, and worship to Him have been the main focus of my life. Service to others is equally as important. I got through a difficult time in my life, because of their service and ministry to me. We cannot make it without each other. We were not designed to walk alone. The church body fits together like a big puzzle. If you want direction, answers, healing, or deliverance in your life, you will find all of that in Christ. If you want to see Him work, you'll see it through His church body.

Ephesians 4:16

From whom the whole body fitly joined together and compacted by that which every joint supplieth, according to the effectual working in the measure of every part, maketh increase of the body unto the edifying of itself in love

So we fit together. We're made for each other. We all need love. We all need to feel we're a part of something greater. God chose us, ordinary people. He uses us with all our faults and shortcomings to demonstrate His love. His true followers and worshipers love like Him, give like Him, and sacrifice like Him. They lay down their needs for their brothers and sisters, and be an extension of His loving, strong arms. That's exactly what Jesus did. He died for mankind. His love is perfect. His mercy unending and His gift is free.

John 15:13

There is no greater love than to lay down one's life for one's friends.

If nothing else, this experience has given me an insatiable desire to be like Christ. I want to return the love shown me during this time in my life. I want to communicate that love to others, so they may know this sense of belonging and wholeness. Our love has limits. When our character and love fall short, we call upon the unending supply of Love from our Heavenly Father. Call on the Lord:

James 4:8

Draw nigh to God, and he will draw nigh to you...

Psalm 145:18

The Lord is nigh unto all them that call upon him,
To all that call upon him in truth

God will never reject anyone, but will lead us to truth. I believe He allows things to happen for our growth and maturity. Through our experiences, we receive strength, courage, and the wisdom to overcome obstacles in our lives. He can put people in our lives to exhibit His love boldly and unselfishly, just like Christ. This truth can lead to total and miraculous deliverance in any area of our lives.

Please don't get discouraged when imposters cross your path. Fight for this priceless heritage of truth and unity God has given through His family. Find a body of believers who will help provide an umbrella of protection to cover you, and help you.

It's one of God's ways to enable you to stand, and present you faultless before the presence of His glory.

Jude 1:24

Now unto him that is able to keep you from falling,
and to present you faultless, Before the presence of his
glory with exceeding joy...

May God give you discernment and help you foresee any danger awaiting you on this journey through life. I pray someone is placed in your life to mirror the love of Christ. Someone who can be an advocate of God's truth, extending the touch of His healing hand. Someone who brings you mercy and wisdom to know how to avoid the pitfalls, or the grace and strength to get you through them. I need you and you need me. Together, we can make it.

I pray my words have successfully painted a clear picture of a loving God who is always there for us. Not only a God who cares, but also a people who care, and reflect His perfect love through their actions and lives. If you've been hurt in the past, don't give up. Keep looking for those who are genuine.

It's difficult to survive by yourself. We weren't designed to live alone, but together as one, supporting and loving each other. When one laughs, we all share the joy. When someone cries, we all share the sorrow and grief. We are intricately bound together.

Because I love music, I equate the family of God to the performance of a great musical composition, skillfully and artistically arranged by the master writer.

The pianist begins with a few light, delicate, and beautiful chords floating through the air, gently massaging listening ears. As the pianist plays, the percussion section begins the pulse, the heartbeat of the music. Not too loud. Like the soft tick of a clock, to keep time in place. Then a rhythm guitar starts strumming notes, mirroring the chords of the piano.

Perhaps the woodwind section is next, chiming in with a whisper of the melody. A soft flute or piccolo is added. Short, staccato notes start to dance on top of the melody. Then the roar of the brass section brings in a full, hearty sound, filling in the measures. Great sounds bellow out, in comparison to the great and mighty winds of a storm.

Slowly, but intricately, one by one, each instrument begins to enter this musical composition with its own distinct sound. All instruments begin to swell as they travel through the piece and reach a great crescendo. Toward the end, the timing of the drum section drives the band with the force of a battle cry, and is solidified with the thunder and crash of cymbals, toms and snare.

Every note helps set the mood, helping to deliver a message and feel and experience the heart of the song. The whole atmosphere vibrates when the stringed bass instrument hits the lowest note on the scale, and ties everything together, ringing total unity into the composition.

When orchestrated perfectly together, it's a masterpiece. The completing factor brings our Lord and Creator the most intense pleasure when He hears the redeemed add their voices and words of praise, admiration, and worship into the concert. It brings the entire strain to a rising climax.

Our lives can be that descriptive and complete when we allow others to add accompaniment and harmony to our lives. Through the amazing process of life we can experience fellowship with each other. We can also enjoy sweet communion with the Holy Spirit.

Miracles and supernatural things happen when the Master has a plan, and inspires men and women to perform it; for our benefit and for His glory. This message of love is crucial for our survival and existence.

It's easy to be consumed with worries and miss a lifetime opportunity to enhance relationships with loved ones. We ignore or misuse the chance to build good, strong, healthy relationships. So devoured by things we think we need to accomplish, the more important things in life are left undone.

We were not designed to live for ourselves, or by ourselves. God had a divine purpose for creating family. If you allow Him to fulfill this purpose in your life, you will be blessed above measure. You're never alone, for God has many extensions called the Body Of Christ. Be inspired to draw closer to God, renew relationships, and learn to reach out in love. Past disappointments, pride, or even low self-esteem can rob us of this special gift and blessing. When you're at your lowest, allow someone in and accept their love and support to lift you to a place of safety. We need each other to survive.

Made in the USA
Charleston, SC
04 December 2014